W9-BTL-160

At Issue

Hybrid and Electric Cars

Other Books in the At Issue Series:

Animal Experimentation

Are Abortion Rights Threatened?

Are Teen Boot Camps Effective?

Are Unions Still Relevant?

Child Pornography

The Children of Undocumented Immigrants

Club Drugs

Digitized Textbooks

Do Cell Phones Cause Cancer?

Fast Food

Fracking

High School Dropouts

How Far Should Science Extend the Human Lifespan?

Is China's Economic Growth a Threat to America?

Reality TV

Road Rage

Should Drilling Be Permitted in the Arctic National Wildlife Refuge?

Should the Rich Pay Higher Taxes?

Should the US Close Its Borders?

Super PACs

What Is the Impact of Twitter?

WikiLeaks

At Issue

I Hybrid and Electric Cars

Louise I. Gerdes, Book Editor

GREENHAVEN PRESS
A part of Gale, Cengage Learning

GALE
CENGAGE Learning·

Farmington Hills, Mich • San Francisco • New York • Waterville, Maine
Meriden, Conn • Mason, Ohio • Chicago

Elizabeth Des Chenes, *Director, Content Strategy*
Douglas Dentino, *Manager, New Product*

For more information, contact:
Greenhaven Press
27500 Drake Rd.
Farmington Hills, MI 48331-3535
Or you can visit our Internet site at gale.cengage.com

LIBRARY OF CONGRESS CATALOGING-IN-PUBLICATION DATA

Hybrid and electric cars / Louise I. Gerdes, book editor.
    pages cm -- (At issue)
   Includes bibliographical references and index.
   ISBN 978-0-7377-6838-1 (hardcover) -- ISBN 978-0-7377-6839-8 (paperback)
   1. Electric automobiles--Juvenile literature. 2. Hybrid electric cars--Juvenile lit-erature. I. Gerdes, Louise I., 1953- editor of compilation.
   TL220.H894 2014
   629.22'93--dc23
                        2014002604

Printed in the United States of America
1 2 3 4 5 6 7 18 17 16 15 14

Contents

Introduction   7

1. Hybrid and Electric Cars Will Reduce   11
   America's Dependence on Petroleum
   Perry Bell

2. Electric Cars Are Not Yet Ready   15
   to Replace Traditional Cars
   Jason Perlow

3. Why Electric Cars Are Cleaner   23
   James Kliesch

4. The Environmental Benefits of Electric   33
   Cars Vary State to State
   *Daniel Yawitz, Alyson Kenward, and
   Eric D. Larson*

5. More Hybrid Vehicles Will Not Fairly   41
   Address Climate Change
   Robert Engelman

6. Electric Cars Make the United States   44
   More Competitive
   Pew Environment Group

7. China Not Embracing Electric Cars   49
   Nathan Bomey

8. Selling Electric Vehicles Like Smartphones   54
   Will Make Them Appealing
   Carl Pope

9. Hybrids Are the Most Economically   58
   Viable Alternative Fuel Vehicles
   Jeremy Michalek, interviewed by Megan McArdle

10. The Government Should Subsidize   69
    Electric Cars
    Nick Chambers

11. The Government Should Not Subsidize   75
    Electric Cars
    Mark J. Perry

12. A Mileage Tax to Replenish Highway   80
    Revenue Is Fair
    Gerald Bastarache

13. A Mileage Tax to Replenish Highway   84
    Revenue Is Unfair
    Ethan Epstein

Organizations to Contact   89

Bibliography   95

Index   100

Introduction

As of October 2013, Americans have purchased a cumulative total of 501,369 hybrid electric vehicles (HEVs) for the year, according to the Electric Drive Transportation Association. Of this total, 423,290 were standard HEVs, while plug-in hybrid electric vehicles (PHEVs) and battery electric vehicles (BEVs) made up the remaining 78,079 vehicles sold. Indeed, HEVs are no longer an uncommon sight on US highways; PHEVs and BEVs, however, are much less common. Although electric vehicles comprised only about 16 percent of the approximately half million HEVs, PHEVs, and BEVs sold thus far in 2013, according to Zachary Shahan of CleanTechnica, electric vehicle sales are up 530 percent from 2012. While still a small percentage of the car market, sales of these vehicles grow each year. The reasons why more Americans buy electric cars each year is varied and complex. Many simply want to save money on the high cost of petroleum fuel. Some want to support economic growth and American jobs in a growing industry. Still others hope to reduce the carbon emissions that contribute to climate change or the security threat posed by our dependence on foreign oil. In truth, many buy electric cars for a combination of these factors. Whether widespread use of these vehicles is in fact the best way to address these concerns is controversial, as the viewpoints in this volume attest. Indeed, while some analysts assert that electric cars will effectively resolve these economic, energy, and environmental concerns, others claim that simply increasing the fuel efficiency of gasoline-powered cars will better address these problems in the near term. Still others argue that a culture shift to car-free living is necessary to truly reduce our dependence on fossil fuels and mitigate the environmental impact of this dependence.

Those who support the widespread use of electric cars argue that these vehicles best serve American interests. "There is a clear national interest in using domestic electricity in our vehicles to reduce dependence on oil, increase energy security, encourage job growth and drive savings at the gas pump,"[1] claims Brian Wynne, president of the Electric Drive Transportation Association. He does not deny that bringing new technologies into the mainstream poses risks. The fact that electric car technology is still developing and widespread consumer acceptance remains unproven is, in Wynne's view, no reason not to support electric cars. In fact, Wynne argues, government support for strategically important but at the time unproven and controversial industries, such as intercontinental railroads and aerospace, was not uncommon. Thus, he praises government efforts to accelerate electric vehicle use. In truth, the Obama administration has set a goal of having one million electric cars on American roads by 2015 and has backed this goal with $5 billion in taxpayer dollars. According to Wynne, "our industry is growing fast, adding jobs throughout the supply chain and selling more vehicles and components than ever."[2] Wynne nevertheless bemoans efforts to attack the industry, lamenting, "The future is bright, but you'd never know it from some of the commentary."[3]

In truth, some commentators claim that Americans are not yet ready to embrace all-electric vehicles. According to Henry Lee, the Jassim M. Jaidah Family Director of the Environment and Natural Resources Program at Harvard University, electric vehicles "could make inroads in 2020 to 2030, but I wouldn't bet on it in the next few years."[4] To reduce oil dependence in the near term, these analysts argue, focusing on

1. Brian Wynne, "Stop Bashing Electric Cars," *Politico*, April 18, 2012. http://www.politico.com/news/stories/0412/75303.html.
2. Ibid.
3. Ibid.
4. Quoted in Jennifer Weeks, "U.S. Oil Dependence," *CQ Researcher*, June 22, 2012. http://photo.pds.org:5012/cqresearcher/document.php?id=cqresrre2012062200#.UwIl9IW9Yic.

fuel efficient gas-powered vehicles makes more sense. Walter McManus, an economist at Oakland University's School of Business Administration in Michigan and a former market analyst at General Motors, does not oppose electric vehicles as a long-term strategy. However, he asserts, "If the goal is to use less fuel now, you can argue that the best way is to keep improving internal combustion engines by ratcheting up fuel economy targets, not by picking a technology."[5] McManus praises the Obama administration's new fuel efficiency standards for US cars and light trucks. The goal of the new standards is to double the fuel efficiency of these vehicles to 54.5 miles per gallon by 2025. McManus sees these standards as a breakthrough that will require manufacturers to make all vehicles more efficient rather than only select cars that they produce. "Manufacturers will have to make everything lighter across their fleets, downsize engines, turbocharge them and add features like stop-start systems. . . . They'll have to address all of the ways that today's cars use energy,"[6] he reasons.

For other analysts, only a major cultural change will reduce oil dependence and the devastating impact of cars on the climate. These activists see the window of opportunity to change planet-altering energy practices closing. Thus, they assert that Americans must reject their dependence on cars. They recommend that rather than drive, Americans should car pool, use public transportation, and bike or walk whenever possible. Culture change activist Jan Lundberg claims that not only can people save money and reduce pollution, they can also pedal their way to health and reduce the number of deaths on America's roads. These activists oppose simply replacing gas-fueled vehicles with electric cars. According to Bill LeBon, who writes for *Culture Change*, an online publication of the Sustainable Energy Institute, "The average car consumes more energy to produce than all the fuel it consumes

5. Quoted in Weeks, op. cit.
6. Ibid.

in its lifetime. Electric cars consume even more."[7] Nevertheless, those who advocate reducing the use of cars claim that environmental organizations such as the Sierra Club are misleading environmentally conscientious American consumers by promoting electric cars. "The cost of a new car generally reflects the energy it consumed to make it, and electric cars are much more expensive than gas cars. Promoting 'green cars' gives people a false impression that car culture can somehow be good,"[8] LeBon argues. Although these activists continue to promote reduced car dependence, they long for the days when environmentalists were a more united community. Lundberg writes, "Somewhere along the line since [the activism of the 1960s and 1970s], money became everything for all but eccentric members of society—as people gave themselves over to the consensus of consuming."[9]

Whether electric cars, increased fuel efficiency standards, or a commitment to reduce driving will resolve the nation's economic, energy, and environmental concerns remains hotly contested. The authors in the following book, *At Issue: Hybrid and Electric Cars*, debate these and other issues surrounding the potential of hybrid and electric cars, their impact, and the policies that best manage their implementation. Despite concerns, hybrid and electric entrepreneurs are optimistic. Writing in *The Futurist*, Jim Motavalli, environmental writer and author of *High Voltage: The Fast Track to Plug In the Auto Industry*, predicts, "Electric cars are going to jumpstart our lives and do good things for the planet, too."[10] Whether this future will become a reality remains to be seen.

7. Quoted in Jan Lundberg, "Sierra Club's Electric Cars: Is It Time for More Technology or Culture Change?," *Culture Change*, April 13, 2012. http://www.culturechange .org/cms/content/view/835/1.
8. Ibid.
9. Ibid.
10. Jim Motavalli, "The Road Ahead for Gasoline-Free Cars," *The Futurist*, March/April 2012.

1

Hybrid and Electric Cars Will Reduce America's Dependence on Petroleum

Perry Bell

Perry Bell is president and chief executive officer of Solar Energy USA, a renewable energy company that specializes in affordable solar powered energy solutions including photovoltaic solar panel systems and electric car charging stations.

Driving plug-in hybrids and, ultimately, all-electric cars will reduce America's dependence on petroleum. Indeed, as battery technology develops and the electric car fuel infrastructure expands, America can meet its demand for fuel with its own supply. In turn, the nation will not have to send people to the Middle East so that other Americans can drive. Overcoming the political influence of those who control traditional fuel sources will be a challenge, but it is not impossible. In truth, one does not have to have to be a liberal or an environmentalist to want the American renewable fuel economy to develop. In the end, those who oppose the evolution to renewable energy sources and electric cars only slow inevitable progress.

What are the real issues of electric cars today? The answer is nothing different from any new technology. If you look at any everyday technological advancement like computers, cell phones, etc., what was once large in size and cost is now smaller and more affordable. The same is true with cars, but one difference to other technologies is that a car's fuel source has been owned by large industries that help support and run our country. This fuel source ownership heavily influences our government to meet their interest—a big hurdle but one that isn't insurmountable. The unique aspect of plug-in hybrids and electric vehicles that threaten the residual fuel economy is the need for electricity instead.

I know that renewable energy and electric cars can help create a better America for ourselves and for future generations.

The Path to Electric Cars

Electric vehicle battery technology is constantly improving and will eventually meet and exceed 100% of any driving desire or need. Plug-in hybrid cars are a great multi-year segway into accommodating infrastructure to support electric cars. The mentality that there is no better way than what we are doing now will not survive ingenuity, and will progress into eventually leaving those who don't grow behind. With a plug-in hybrid, you can recharge (refuel) at home or only when you want and not have limitations because the car is a hybrid with great fuel efficiency when not using an electric charge. You could drive within the electric range and seldom ever use petroleum fuel. No matter what you do, this will dramatically reduce the current demand for petroleum. And while this is happening, the same battery that only went 40 miles last year will now go 60 miles just one year later. That cycle will eventually be a number that doesn't limit someone's journey, just like anyone who needs a gas station today.

People are creatures of habit. If you look at where you drive on a daily and weekly basis, with few exceptions, there is a great deal of consistency. There is a point and range that will make sense for you if that point is not already currently available. I write this message from experience of driving a plug-in hybrid for the last year and a half. Also, I travel with a non-plug-in hybrid and I race petroleum fueled cars. My goal isn't environmental, though that is a great byproduct. My decision revolves around independence and financial logic.

Serving Demand with Our Own Supply

I'm writing this article as a republican embarrassed that the leftwing is leading the charge in progress, which is the backbone of this country, without financial guidance. The only brainwashed response I hear from my voting group is that it is not viable and we should explore something else. I do not want to put the oil workers out of work, but the current situation is no different than the blacksmith or farrier who put horseshoes on horses when the car came along—that occupation evolved into being a mechanic. I also don't want to send friends and family members to the Middle East just so I can fill up my car. If Americans reduce our need for petroleum enough, we can service our own demand with our current supply.

The political decisions based around petroleum and our country's need for fuel is unhealthy. As an individual, I can create my own fuel for my plug-in hybrid through solar technology at my house, which I do, and I can also use solar energy to offset my electricity usage from the power company. Comparing the cost of petroleum against the cost of my solar system (without any incentives) gives me a 2.5 year payback. At that point, my plug-in hybrid's fuel source is free. As you can see, solar power has the potential to be a disruptive technology, and this can be a problem for our country's residual revenue with respect to political special interests. However, it may not be as bad as it seems once things evolve.

Like many others in America you may wait for the answers, but I already have mine. I know that renewable energy and electric cars can help create a better America for ourselves and for future generations.

2

Electric Cars Are Not Yet Ready to Replace Traditional Cars

Jason Perlow

Jason Perlow, technology editor at ZDNet, integrates multi-vendor computing environments for Fortune 500 companies and is currently a technology strategist with Microsoft Corporation.

Electric cars are not yet ready to replace gasoline-powered vehicles in the American marketplace. In fact, sales of electric vehicles (EVs) for most automakers have been poor. One key reason is that the range of EVs is relatively short and thus useful only for local driving. Also, people who support EVs as a means of reducing fossil fuel dependence should remember that, in many cases, fossil fuels generate the electricity that charges EVs. If the country truly wants to shift from fossil fuels, policy makers should consider other sources of energy, such as nuclear and biodiesel. Indeed, if EVs are to be a viable technology and replace fossil fuels, people must address broader energy concerns.

I like the idea of electric cars. Heck, I've driven them, and downright enjoyed doing so. The inner geek within me yearns for a car that makes no noise other than a suppressed electric whine, and that glides down the highway like something out of a futuristic sci-fi movie or *Knight Rider*.[1]

---

1. *Knight Rider* was a 1980s television show, in which the show's protagonist, Michael Knight, played by David Hasselhoff, was assisted by a highly advanced, artificially intelligent car.

Jason Perlow, "Electric Cars and Plug-in Hybrids Are a Fail," *ZDNet*, May 27, 2013. Copyright © 2013 by ZDNet.com. All rights reserved. Reproduced by permission.

So let's just get this out of the way: *I do not hate electric cars.* In fact I think they are awesomely cool, and are an incredible technical achievement.

That being said, at this stage of their technical development, and given other issues related to the production of electricity in this and in many other countries, I don't think they are even close to being ready for prime time.

Poor Electric Vehicle Sales

In the last year [2012] we've seen various aspects of the EV [electric vehicle] ecosystem self-destruct. GM's Volt sales have been so awful that the company decided to temporarily suspend production of the car in the spring of last year for over a month and had to issue heavy discounts to move inventory.

To be kind as well as factually correct, GM sold over 23,000 Volts in 2012, which is triple what it did in 2011, but that isn't saying an awful lot.

If you compare the total sales of the Volt to date with the vehicle that shares its platform, the top-selling compact car in North America—the Chevy Cruze—it's so small that it's practically a rounding error. Approximately 237,000 Cruzes were sold in 2012, and 231,000 in 2011.

Yes, there have been about 14 Chevy Cruzes sold for every Volt sold to date. Even if you factor in that about a quarter of all Cruzes go to rental car agencies, the consumer sales gap between GM's electric vehicle sales and comparable gasoline-based car sales is staggering.

And it's not just GM that can't seem to make significant headway with EVs. Nissan's Leaf failed to make even 10,000 deliveries in the US in 2012. The company is doing a bit better this year, but these numbers are certainly not significant by any means. The company hit the total US sales milestone of 25,000 cars this month, again after over a $6000 price cut before federal incentives.

And those are the electric cars that are doing *well-ish*.

Just in the last few months, both CODA Automotive, an electric car company and EV battery manufacturer, as well as A123 Systems, another battery manufacturer have filed for bankruptcy protection.

Fisker Automotive, the producer of the exotic Karma plug-in electric hybrid sports car who hired the former head of GM's Volt division, Tony Posawatz, to be its CEO, just fired almost all of its staff and is preparing for total asset liquidation after producing about 2,000 vehicles total.

[Tesla] is doing well, but it's the only maker of electric vehicles and related products that is doing well.

Better Place, which was a Palo Alto and Israeli-based start-up that tried to create an international subscriber network of charging stations for EVs ceased operations this week, after burning through approximately $700 millon of capital from multiple seed investors since beginning their venture funding in 2010.

Exceptions to the Rule

I'm sure you Elon Musk fans are just raring at the bit to tell me that Tesla has exceeded Wall Street expectations for Q1 in 2013. True, the company is doing well, but it's the *only* maker of electric vehicles and related products that is doing well.

If anything, Tesla has simply validated its place as the automotive equivalent of Apple, as a high-end luxury products maker for the eco-savvy nouveau riche. The company has sold about 5,000 of its $70,000+ cars to date. It also has an extremely wealthy benefactor, who has diversified into other industries such as commercial space vehicles, and can treat the business like an expensive hobby.

I'm going to treat Tesla as an exception to the rule. As a whole, people don't want electric cars. Oh, don't get me wrong, they like the *idea* and the *philosophy* behind electric cars, but push comes to shove, your average middle class person who can afford to buy a new car doesn't want to own an EV.

It's also true that hybrids have gotten quite a bit of success in the last decade, such as the (regular) Toyota Prius and Honda's various hybrid offerings.

Not only is your average middle class family unable to afford a $70,000 Tesla Model S, but they also can't afford to buy a $38,000 Chevy Volt, or a $35,000 Nissan Leaf, even after government incentives.

I don't consider hybrids true EVs, though, as they employ regenerative methods using their gasoline engines and braking systems to power a relatively small battery pack, which is only used a fraction of the time, and they still have mechanical linkages to the drivetrain from the gasoline motor.

The Volt, Fisker and one of the latest variations of the Prius are "Plug-in" hybrid EVs, in the sense that they rely on their battery packs first, and then kick in their gasoline engines to power the electric drivetrain when the batteries completely expend their range, which for the Volt is about 50 miles.

The Nissan Leaf and the Tesla Model S are pure EVs— they only rely on their batteries to run and require the use of charging stations on extended trips. The Leaf can go for about 75–100 miles between charges and the Tesla Model S can go up to (an impressive) 265 miles before a recharge.

The Problem with EVs

Let's summarize why these cars don't make sense. First, *they cost a lot of money*. Not only is your average middle class family unable to afford a $70,000 Tesla Model S, but they also can't afford to buy a $38,000 Chevy Volt, or a $35,000 Nissan Leaf, even after government incentives, when a comparable Cruze or a Sentra costs half the amount of money.

GM will shortly be releasing the Spark EV, a sub-compact, lower priced pure electric vehicle with an 82-mile range that will cost about $27,500 before federal tax credits. This is still probably too much money for an EV, especially such a small one with such limited range.

We don't really know, long-term, how these exotic batteries and other parts in EVs are going to perform as these vehicles age, and what the longer-term maintenance costs will be.

And we're not even getting into pre-owned vehicles as potential competition here. New car sales, as a whole, pretty much suck.

You could make the argument that charging these cars with electricity from your home is cheaper than filling the tank, but how long is that going to take you to make up twice the cost of a comparable gasoline vehicle?

Second is the issue of range. While the Tesla is indeed an impressive performer at a luxury price, the Volt (if you treat it strictly as an EV) and the Leaf essentially are only good for local driving.

Then there is the issue of long-term reliability and safety. We don't really know, long-term, how these exotic batteries and other parts in EVs are going to perform as these vehicles age, and what the longer-term maintenance costs will be.

We understand what to expect from fossil fuel engines because they've been around for over 100 years, and there's a hugely established parts and repair infrastructure industry surrounding it. Not so for EVs.

Now, you could also make the argument that EVs aren't all about saving money, it's about making yourself feel good, knowing you can live a greener lifestyle. I dig that.

But the only way you're really going to live a greener lifestyle is to go completely off the grid, which means investing in (expensive) solar panels, wind and water turbines, and collecting an energy surplus using big capacitive batteries and power inverters to juice your EV with.

Otherwise, all that you are doing is juicing your car with electricity that is created largely by fossil fuel-burning power plants from your metropolitan power infrastructure.

Looking at Alternative Fuel Sources

So if we really want to get rid of non-renewable fuel sources, not only do we have to get it out of our cars, but we have to get it out of our municipal power plants.

If we want to be independent from the oil-producing nations, then we need to start thinking creatively.

And guess what—the best alternative to this is nuclear energy, [which] is the greenest, most efficient electric power producing system of all. Don't beleive me? You might want to catch *Pandora's Promise.* . . .

I'm not going to get into the political ramifications and NIMBYism [not in my backyardism] of nuclear energy. Nor will I lay out an economic model which would prove that building out large scale nuclear power infrastructure would result in the creation of *millions* of new jobs.

Instead, let's talk about other forms of renewable, sustainable fuel sources for cars.

The modern hybrid vehicle, be it a conventional regenerative design like a Prius or a plug-in like a Chevy Volt still uses gasoline for the conventional part of its powertrain. If we want to be independent from the oil-producing nations, then we need to start thinking creatively.

We have a potential fuel source and propulsion technology that will solve our sustainability as well as greatly reduce our dependence on oil producing countries for automotive fuel and other petroleum needs.

It's proven, with over 100 years of maturity, and its use would not require a major re-tooling of our automotive manufacturing capabilities.

That fuel is *Diesel*. Specifically, Biodiesel and Biomass to Liquid (BTL) diesel fuel.

Today, most diesel cars run on fuel that comes from petroleum derivatives. But they can also run on fuels based on vegetable and plant oils. I drive a Chattanooga, Tennesee-built 2012 Volkswagen Passat TDI that in a pinch, could actually run on pure vegetable oil if I needed it to, Volkswagen's warranty terms notwithstanding.

My Passat TDI gets on the average of about 600 miles to the tank with mixed city and highway driving in Florida with the A/C system running whenever I drive. In various driving scenarios the car can actually achieve over 800 miles per tank, especially if you are doing mostly highway driving.

There have even been verified stories of people getting 1600 miles to a tank with this car, under careful driving conditions.

Reallocating Resources

What if we reallocated much of the farmland that is producing corn—that is being used to produce the very same high-fructose corn syrup (HFCS) which is permeating virtualy every processed food product sold today and that is creating an obesity and diabetes epedemic [sic] in this country?

What if we used most of those corn fields to produce, say, marijuana or industrial hemp instead? Or grow it in areas where food crops cannot thrive?

Without getting into cannabis's psychoactive and medicinal properties and also as a potential taxable revenue source if legalized for recreational use, the industrial variants of hemp would be excellent renewable sources for biodiesel/BTL production.

And as a by-product of a large biodiesel industry, hemp would yield extremely durable fibers for all sorts of applications (including apparel and plastics) as well as excellent and healthy cooking oils and food protein. And think about the jobs these industries would create.

Pure electric vehicles might be viable someday. Unfortunately, that day may be a decade or more away. But before we even attempt to popularize them we need to figure out how to solve the overall sustainable energy problem using conventional technology, while keeping vehicle and fuel costs down.

3

Why Electric Cars Are Cleaner

James Kliesch

James Kliesch is a senior engineer at the nonprofit Union of Concerned Scientists and an expert in advanced and clean vehicle technologies. He is also a contributing editor to Mother Earth News, *a magazine that promotes sustainable living.*

Electric cars benefit the environment in many ways. Electric cars produce zero emissions from the tailpipe. Moreover, while electric cars do produce some pollution in the manufacturing process and in parts of the nation that use fossil fuels to generate electricity, on a national average, electric cars produce half the amount of carbon dioxide as a conventional car. Although gas-powered cars produce fewer pollutants than in the past, they still produce significant amounts of carbon dioxide, which contributes to global warming. In fairness, electric cars do produce carbon dioxide in parts of the country, such as the midwest, where electricity is generated from coal. However, in the northeast, northwest, and Pacific coast, where electricity is generated from hydroelectric sources, electric cars are much cleaner. Thus, as power generation becomes cleaner nationwide so will electric cars.

As of 2011, the electric car is no longer a hypothetical car of the future. Thanks to unveilings from major automakers, corporate investment, dedicated government backing and steady improvements to the technology itself, electric cars are ready to claim a spot as a car of the present. It's been quite a ride. After first appearing in the early 1900s and then flirting with a return in the 1990s, electric cars (sometimes called EVs, for electric vehicles) fell back to niche status. But recent history has seen nearly the entire auto industry recharge about electric cars. Some notable buzz:

- General Motors is back in the game with production of the Chevy Volt, a plug-in hybrid capable of traveling 25 to 50 miles on electricity alone. The Volt has already won several notable awards, including the *Motor Trend* 2011 Car of the Year and the 2011 Green Car of the Year from *Green Car Journal.*

- Toyota is working on a small electric car, the FT-EV II, and has bought a significant stake in electric car specialist Tesla Motors, maker of the electric Roadster sports car. Tesla and Toyota are developing an electric version of Toyota's RAV4, a small SUV.

- Nissan sold out the preorder waiting list for its all-electric Leaf sedan in 2010, and the car is expected to go on sale nationwide for about $25,000 (after tax credits) by the end of 2011.

- Honda plans to sell its Fit EV, which will have a 70-mile driving range, in 2012.

- Mitsubishi plans to bring its electric compact car, the i-MiEV, to U.S. showrooms by the end of 2011.

- Fisker Automotive, maker of the luxury Karma sedan, received a $529 million federal loan to help develop its plug-in hybrid vehicles.

This resurgence is a testament to recent advances in electric car technology. While pure electric cars will continue to face challenges—such as expensive batteries, a limited driving range compared with conventional cars (although the 70 to 100 miles per charge offered by most electric cars is sufficient for many drivers), somewhat lengthy charging times, and a limited number of public recharging stations—they bring numerous benefits to the table.

Because electric cars consume no gasoline at all, they are a great option for drivers concerned with energy security and our nation's oil dependence. They offer the convenience of being able to "refuel" a vehicle at home, and they're more efficient and less expensive to operate compared with gas-only cars. They also reduce noise pollution in most driving circumstances. Finally, of course, they're perhaps best known for being zero-emission vehicles, and their lack of tailpipe emissions is a great step toward an improved environment.

Electric car emissions depend on multiple factors—particularly how your electricity is generated, which, for most, depends on where you live.

Hold it right there, say some critics. Aren't electric cars simply moving emissions from the vehicle's tailpipe to a power plant smokestack? (This is the "long tailpipe" critique.) Aren't there still greenhouse gas emissions and other pollutants associated with creating the electricity these vehicles use? And if that's the case, are electric cars *really* all they're cracked up to be?

"These are valid questions deserving of a thorough assessment," says Bill Moore, editor in chief of EV World, a transportation technology and news website. While lamenting misinformation that perpetuates in the blogosphere and elsewhere, Moore values criticism that encourages progress. "We don't want [electric cars] to become a burden on society, so we need to hear those criticisms, we need to weigh them, and we need to move forward to improve the technology," he says.

Electric car emissions depend on multiple factors—particularly how your electricity is generated, which, for most, depends on where you live. Smog-forming pollution at the power plant from the use of an electric car can have higher emissions rates than typical gas-only or hybrid cars (such as the Toyota Prius), a fact owed largely to the effectiveness of catalytic converters in today's gas cars. It's important to note, though, that from a health standpoint, one major advantage of "moving" pollution from the tailpipe to the power plant is that it gets pollutants farther away from pedestrians and other drivers, lowering the pollutants' adverse health impacts on the concentrated population.

However, some pollutants, such as those related to climate change, affect the environment regardless of where they are released. In terms of climate change emissions, electric cars are generally much cleaner than conventional gas vehicles. In areas of the country that have the cleanest power generation (more wind, solar and hydropower), electric cars emit far less greenhouse gases, not only compared with conventional vehicles, but also compared with efficient hybrid-electric vehicles. In areas of the country with the dirtiest power generation (coal), an efficient hybrid may be your best environmental bet, though if you're gentle on the pedal, an electric car may yield comparable results. On a national average basis, an efficient electric car emits about half the amount of carbon dioxide as a conventional car, and roughly the same amount as an efficient hybrid. To fully understand these comparisons, we first need to understand the how, what and where of vehicle emissions.

Vehicle Emissions Explained

The vast majority of cars and trucks on today's roads operate on internal combustion engines, which convert energy stored in a liquid fuel (usually gasoline) into mechanical motion by rapidly igniting an air-fuel mixture in the engine's cylinders. This combustion process emits engine exhaust that contains a number of pollutants, including (but not limited to) carbon monoxide, hydrocarbons, nitrogen oxides and particulate matter. But automotive engineers have found ways to reduce these pollutants, both by adding emissions-control devices (such as catalytic converters) to the exhaust plumbing, and by precisely rendering the cylinders' combustion process though computer control. The upshot is that, especially over the past decade, conventional vehicles have gotten much cleaner in terms of smog-forming pollution.

The bad news is that another pollutant created by combusting fuel—carbon dioxide, or CO_2—cannot be minimized through the use of emissions-control devices. Simply put, the more fuel your vehicle burns, the more CO_2 it emits. This is particularly troublesome because CO_2 is the primary human-caused greenhouse gas, contributing heavily to global warming. While a comparison of conventional vehicles and electric cars could be conducted for each of the major pollutants, the critical environmental issue today is the impact our vehicles have on global warming, which is why our calculations focus on CO_2 emissions.

Unlike vehicles with internal combustion engines, electric cars have zero in-use emissions.

A vehicle's emissions can be categorized into three types: in-use, upstream and vehicle-manufacturing emissions. In-use emissions—those produced when someone is actually driving the vehicle—constitute the majority of a typical car's lifetime emissions. Upstream emissions are those that result from producing and transporting the fuel a car uses to its point of use (in the case of gasoline, that means extracting crude oil, refining it and transporting it to gas stations). The third category is manufacturing-related emissions, which, according to the latest research, only account for about 10 to 20 percent of a vehicle's lifetime greenhouse gas output. (Given the modest impact of manufacturing emissions, calculations made in this article include only in-use and upstream emissions.)

Remarkably, burning 1 gallon of gasoline pushes more than 19 pounds of CO_2 out of your vehicle's tailpipe. One gallon of gasoline weighs only about 6 pounds, but the combustion process pulls in oxygen atoms from the surrounding air when creating carbon dioxide. But that's not all. In addition to those 19 pounds of CO_2, nearly another 5 pounds of CO_2 are produced "upstream" during the creation and transportation of that gallon of gas from the wellhead to the refinery to the corner station, all before being put in the car's tank. All told, our cars are responsible for emitting nearly 25 pounds of CO_2 for every gallon of gas they burn.

Unlike vehicles with internal combustion engines, electric cars have zero in-use emissions. They do, however, have upstream emissions: those resulting from producing the vehicle's fuel—in this case, the vehicle's electricity.

Comparing Electrons

When it comes to electricity, the resource used to generate it plays a major role in determining how environmentally friendly its electrons are. The cleanest type of electricity is that generated from renewable energy sources, such as solar, wind and hydropower. Such sources create electricity without producing greenhouse gases or smog-forming pollutants at a power plant. Electric cars powered by electricity created from renewable sources are, for all intents and purposes, true zero-emission vehicles.

Electricity generated by natural gas plants falls in the middle of the pack. It's cleaner than coal power, but not nearly as climate-friendly as power generated from renewable sources.

The worst electricity, from both a global warming and a smog-forming emissions standpoint, comes from coal-fired power plants. They emit the highest levels of carbon dioxide and, depending on the quality of the emissions-control devices on the plants, can emit high levels of smog-forming and toxic emissions as well, including particulate matter (soot).

Nuclear plants, while not a threat from a global warming or smog-forming pollution standpoint, pose the dangerous threats of nuclear disasters and nuclear proliferation. Safe, long-term storage of nuclear waste is also a serious concern. Because of these issues, nuclear energy isn't considered by many (including myself) to be an eco-friendly option at this time.

The cleanliness of your electricity determines how eco-friendly it would be to operate an electric car.

Today, coal-fired power plants generate the majority of electricity in the United States (48 percent), followed by natural gas (22 percent), nuclear (19 percent) and renewables (9 percent). The efficiency of the power plant also affects the eco-friendliness of the electricity it generates. Some plants, such as combined heat and power facilities, make better use of waste energy, which reduces the amount of fuel necessary (and thus pollution emitted) to produce a given amount of energy. The cleanliness of power plant emissions is also tied to what pollution-control technology the plant utilizes. Plants can use scrubbers, for example, to control sulfur emissions. Short of still-unvalidated carbon capture and storage processes, however, there is no method for controlling CO_2 emissions from power plants.

Different U.S. regions utilize vastly different electricity sources. The Northeast, Northwest and Pacific Coast generate electricity using large amounts of renewable hydroelectric power, while the Midwest uses a significant amount of coal.

What does all of this mean for the typical electricity consumer? In short, it means the cleanliness of your electricity determines how eco-friendly it would be to operate an electric car. For example, if you live in California, which has some of the cleanest electricity in the nation, an electric car driven 12,000 miles (a typical year's worth of driving) would emit about 1.6 tons of CO_2. By contrast, a hybrid such as the Toyota Prius would emit about 2.9 tons, and a 25-mpg gas car would emit about 5.9 tons per year. If you live in the Midwest, where coal is king, your electric car's annual emissions would be about 4.1 tons of CO_2—more than that of an efficient hybrid, but still far less than that from a gas-only vehicle.

So, how do the numbers shake out for the rest of the country? The U.S. Department of Energy tracks power plant emissions in more than a dozen different regions and subregions across the nation. This regional emissions information is a good starting point for estimating the environmental impact of electric cars in different regions of the country. Making subsequent calculations to account for regional transmission and distribution losses, vehicle charging equipment losses, and estimated impacts of energy extraction, transportation and processing, it's possible to estimate average electric car emissions around the country.

Today's electric cars are indeed responsible for some pollution, but nevertheless are a cleaner option than most other cars currently on the market.

Another factor to consider is that, while power plants have multiple-decade lifetimes, emissions from the grid are not static. In time, electric cars have the potential to get even cleaner if concerted efforts are made to clean up our energy portfolio with cleaner fossil fuels (natural gas) and, far better yet, even more renewable energy. Each year, the U.S. Department of Energy projects how grid emissions are likely to change in the future. It predicts an electric car driven in California in 2035 will have 39 percent less annual CO_2 emissions than an electric car driven today, and an electric car driven in the East Central region . . . will have 9 percent less annual CO_2 emissions. While constructive on a general level, this information should be viewed cautiously because of the many assumptions that go into such predictions.

A Bright Future for Electric Cars

Electric cars are clearly cleaner than most other vehicles on the road today, but how large of a role can they play in cutting down our transportation sector's greenhouse gas emissions? That depends in part on how many are sold. Unfortunately, predicting the size of the future electric car market is difficult at best. "If you did a Google search on this, you'd see a million hits with a million different answers," says Mark Peny, director of product planning for Nissan North America and a key player behind the Nissan Leaf.

Citing internal market research, a government committed to advanced vehicle technologies, and greater public awareness of the ills of oil dependence, Perry is optimistic, predicting electric cars could account for 10 percent of new vehicles sold by 2020. Analysts at the other end of the spectrum suggest numbers as low as 0.5 percent in that time frame. Forecasting aside, one thing's for certain: Building a successful electric car market will require technological advances, thoughtful infrastructure development, and supportive federal, state and municipal policies.

"There are a bunch of things colliding here," Moore says, and it's "very, very hard" to know how the market will unfold. But he's confident that electric vehicle technology will succeed in time. If that happens, he's correct that it's important to answer difficult questions about the technology sooner rather than later. With that in mind, we revisit our initial question: Do electric cars truly deserve their environmentally friendly reputation, even if accounting for power plant emissions? On a national average basis, the answer today is a firm yes. Today's electric cars are indeed responsible for some pollution, but nevertheless are a cleaner option than most other cars currently on the market. And if we increase our use of renewable energy, the future for electric cars will only get brighter.

4

The Environmental Benefits of Electric Cars Vary State to State

Daniel Yawitz, Alyson Kenward, and Eric D. Larson

Daniel Yawitz is a research analyst at Princeton University's Climate Central, a research organization that studies issues related to climate change. Alyson Kenward manages the research program and Eric D. Larson leads energy-related research at Climate Central. Larson is also part of the research faculty at the Princeton Environmental Institute.

The environmental impact of an electric car varies significantly from state to state. Indeed, how states generate the electricity that charges the car's battery impacts whether an electric vehicle is climate friendly—emitting fewer of the greenhouse gases that lead to global warming. In fact, in some states such as Kentucky and Wyoming, which rely primarily on coal to generate electricity, a fuel efficient gasoline-powered car may be better for the climate. As electricity generation becomes less dependent on fossil fuels such as coal, electric vehicles will better reduce the impact of driving on the environment. Indeed, such reduction has already had an impact. While in 2012, in a majority of states, the hybrid produced fewer emissions than the electric car, in 2013 the all-electric vehicle became more climate friendly.

In April 2012, Climate Central released its first Roadmap to Climate Friendly Cars, a state-by-state analysis of greenhouse gas emissions from electric and gasoline vehicles. Our analysis showed that the electricity used to charge a 2012 Nissan Leaf—advertised as a "zero-emissions" car—actually resulted in more greenhouse gas emissions per mile driven than driving an equivalent high-efficiency gas-powered vehicle in 32 states because of the carbon intensity of the electrical grid.

A Changing Landscape

Last year, our analysis of electric vehicles focused on the new 2012 model-year Leaf and plug-in hybrid Chevrolet Volt. This year, with many more electric and plug-in hybrid cars on the market and some dramatic changes in our nation's electricity generation mix, our analysis reveals a changing landscape for consumers looking to make climate-friendly car choices. . . .

In recent years, about one third of U.S. greenhouse gas emissions have come from the transportation sector and pollution from cars, pickups, SUVs and minivans make up the majority of transportation emissions (Bureau of Transportation Statistics, 2012). While electric vehicles can help play a role in reducing transportation emissions, our analysis finds that they may not be the most climate-friendly option today for many drivers in the U.S.

The total greenhouse gas emissions per mile driven for an electric car depend on *where you live*. Since electric cars draw their power by charging from the electric grid, the carbon-intensity of the source of the electricity, which varies from state to state, has a big impact. . . .

How Electricity Is Generated

How climate friendly an electric car is depends to a large extent on where you live and how electricity is generated in your state. . . . In some states, where low-emission forms of electricity predominate, electric cars emit less climate pollution than conventional gas-powered cars during driving and charging. In states that depend heavily on fossil fuels like coal and natural gas for electricity, there are gas-powered cars that are more climate friendly during driving and charging than electric cars.

Charging and driving a Nissan Leaf produces fewer greenhouse gas emissions than driving a Toyota Prius in 32 states.

When we refer to driving and charging emissions . . . , we are excluding emissions associated with manufacturing the car, but we are including emissions associated with production of the fossil fuels from which gasoline or electricity are produced as well as with combustion of the fuels. . . .

Our analysis pertains only to charging of car batteries with electricity from the grid, which is the way most electric cars are charged today. Charging batteries from another source, such as a roof-top solar panel, would require a separate analysis from that presented here.

Comparing Electric and Hybrid Cars

As it was in 2012, the 2013 Nissan Leaf is still the most efficient electric car on the market (tied with the Honda Fit Electric, excluding two-passenger subcompact cars). . . . Toyota Prius [is] the most fuel-efficient gas-powered car comparable in size to the Leaf. . . .

Charging and driving a Nissan Leaf produces fewer greenhouse gas emissions than driving a Toyota Prius in 32 states, when manufacturing emissions are not included. In 18 states, making electricity generates enough climate pollution that charging and driving a "zero-emissions" Nissan Leaf in those states is worse for the climate than driving a gasoline-powered Prius.

Driving a Prius produces about 0.52 pounds of carbon dioxide equivalents (CO_2e) every mile.

The largest state-to-state differences in emissions for electric vehicles are due to the large differences in carbon-intensity of electricity production that arise from the different mix of electricity generation sources from state-to-state. In states where electricity generation is much more carbon intensive than the national average, the Leaf can produce as much as 0.76 pounds of CO_2e per mile (in Kentucky). And in states with much cleaner electricity than on average in the U.S. the emissions produced per mile are comparably smaller.

In states where electricity generation relies primarily on coal, . . . several fuel-efficient gasoline-powered cars are better for the climate than electrics or plug-in hybrids.

While there are 18 states where charging and driving the gas-powered Prius produces fewer emissions than the electric Leaf, the Leaf is still far more climate friendly than the average new gas-powered car in any state. The average new vehicle in 2012 got about 25 miles per gallon and produced more than 1 pound of CO_2e for every mile driven, or twice the emissions of a Prius.

MPG Fuel Economy

Another way to compare emissions of electric and gas-power cars is to calculate the mpg fuel economy that a gas-powered car would need to have in order to be more climate friendly than a particular electric car. This could be called the equivalent MPG fuel economy for the electric car in question, and it would change with the carbon-intensity of the electricity used by the electric car.

Where the electrical grid is the least carbon intensive, including Washington, Idaho, and Oregon, a gas-powered vehicle would need fuel efficiencies of at least 200 miles per gallon to beat the Leaf. In Vermont, a conventional car would need to get over 2,600 miles per gallon to be more climate-friendly than the Leaf.

In states where electricity generation relies primarily on coal, or on a majority of coal and natural gas, several fuel-efficient gasoline-powered cars are better for the climate than electrics or plug-in hybrids. In states like Kentucky, Indiana, and Wyoming, for example, gas-powered cars only need to have fuel efficiencies of 34 37 miles per gallon to be the most climate-friendly options for drivers. In those states, there are many cars on the market that would be a better choice for the climate than an electric car.

If an electric car charges in a state like West Virginia (96 percent coal) or Kentucky (92 percent coal), the greenhouse gas emissions from driving will be higher than driving the car in a state with little-to-no coal and natural gas.

Climate-friendly Plug-in Hybrids

Plug-in hybrid vehicles can also be a climate-friendly vehicle choice. These cars can be charged and run exclusively on electricity, so in states with low carbon intensity electricity generation, can be a cleaner option than the most fuel-efficient gas-powered cars. However, the distance that plug-in hybrids can travel solely on electricity before gasoline assist is needed tends to be short, at around 10–40 miles.

Where electricity generation is not carbon intensive, a plug-in hybrid in our analysis will produce fewer emissions from driving than a nonplug-in hybrid, but the plug-in hybrid will produce more emissions from driving than most cars that run exclusively on electricity. On the other hand, where electricity generation is very carbon intensive plug-in hybrids may produce fewer emissions than an all-electric car, but more emissions than a fuel-efficient gas-powered car. Because a plug-in hybrid runs partially on electricity and partially on gasoline, its greenhouse gas emissions depend on the mix of miles driven using electricity versus miles driven using gasoline. For our analysis we assume half the miles are driven on electricity and half on gasoline. . . .

Electricity Generation, State-by-State

The variations in electric vehicle driving emissions between states come from the large differences in how electricity is produced from state to state. . . . Each state has a unique mix of electricity generation, which means electricity in each state also has a different average carbon emissions intensity. Fossil fuels used for generating electricity, and especially coal, play a key role. In 2012, coal was used to generate the largest share of electricity in the U.S. as a whole, followed by natural gas.

To make the calculations tractable, our analysis assumes that charging a car battery in a given state uses electricity with a carbon intensity equal to the annual average carbon emissions intensity of electricity generated in that state. There are uncertainties associated with this assumption, because it is difficult to determine with accuracy where an electron goes once it enters the grid (e.g., it may cross a state line) and because the carbon intensity of electricity generation within a state changes on an hourly or shorter basis as the level of electricity demand changes and different power generating sources start up or shut down to accommodate the changes. . . .

With our assumptions, if an electric car charges in a state like West Virginia (96 percent coal) or Kentucky (92 percent coal), the greenhouse gas emissions from driving will be higher than driving the car in a state with little-to-no coal and natural gas. In a state that instead relies heavily on nuclear power, hydropower, and renewables like wind and solar power, there are very few emissions during electricity generation. Vermont, for example, generated nearly 75 percent of its electricity from nuclear power, and Washington made 76 percent of its electricity at hydroelectric dams, and these are the top states in which electric cars are the most climate-friendly options.

Decreasing Coal Consumption

For the U.S. as a whole from 2010 to 2012, the fraction of electricity generated from coal dropped to 37 percent from 45 percent. Electricity from natural gas increased by more than 6 percentage points to 30.5 percent, driven by natural gas prices that reached a 10-year low in 2012. Wind and solar power growth accounted for the rest of the coal power reduction over this period.

In some states, changes in coal and natural gas-powered electricity generation were much more pronounced than at the national level. For example, Delaware saw its share of electricity coming from coal drop by 30 percentage points while the share coming from natural gas rose by 27 percentage points. Alabama, Massachusetts, Maryland, Montana, North Carolina, Ohio, Virginia, and Wisconsin all saw coal power drop by at least 10 percentage points.

In most states, the decrease in coal consumption was largely met with increased use of natural gas, but increasing renewable energy, including hydro, wind and solar power, also helped make up the difference. Washington, Oregon, and Montana each saw the share of hydropower increase by about 10 percent, and South Dakota and Iowa both saw the share of electricity from wind power increase by at least 8 percent.

Our 2012 report *A Roadmap to Climate-Friendly Cars*, which was based on 2010 electricity generation data, showed that in 36 states, the high mileage gas-powered Toyota Prius (2012 model) produced fewer overall driving emissions than the all-electric 2012 Nissan Leaf. As noted above, this year the trend has essentially reversed; in 32 states, the all-electric 2013 Leaf is more climate friendly than the 2013 Prius considering only the driving and charging emissions. Our analysis represents only a snapshot of the grid in time. As the carbon intensity of the grid changes in the future, the per-mile emissions calculated for all-electric and plug-in electric hybrid will change.

5

More Hybrid Vehicles Will Not Fairly Address Climate Change

Robert Engelman

Robert Engelman is vice president for programs at the World-watch Institute, an environmental research organization based in Washington, DC.

Driving more hybrids will not solve the global climate change problem. In fact, if every person on earth drove a hybrid, the problem of global warming would only intensify. In reality, all driving that emits greenhouse gases should be reduced. However, few people in developing nations drive. Indeed, America continues to emit more greenhouse gases than most other nations. Nevertheless, political entities determine climate policy despite the fact that the impact of emissions knows no political boundaries. To fairly address climate change, the United States and other high-emitting nations must take the lead to reduce emissions and help finance emission reduction in developing nations.

"Theoretically, it seats 6.75 billion," the ad for the new Honda Insight hybrid car states.

My first thought when encountering this ad in *TIME* magazine was that it plays to a pretty narrow demographic; people who know that this big number is the current population of the world. Then I read the ad copy.

Honda's ad evokes one thought that ought to dominate the discussion at the international climate change conference in Copenhagen, Denmark, this December [2009]: Global development is inequitable. Some of us worry about the mileage our car gets. But most people don't own, drive, or ride in any car, let alone a hybrid.

On the one hand, Honda is playing to a sense of fairness that its American audience may have. "Sure," the typical magazine reader might think. "Everyone should drive a hybrid. Good for Honda." Yet even a fuel-efficient hybrid car could be disastrous for the planet.

"The more hybrid drivers, the better," the ad declares unambiguously. "For all of us."

Really?

More Drivers Are Not Better

If 6.75 billion people drive vehicles that get 42 miles per gallon 10,000 miles a year, what happens to oil supplies and energy prices? To roads and open space? More importantly, what happens to the atmosphere? Honda might be more responsible spreading the message that those who feel they must drive should downshift to a more efficient model, maybe an Insight.

It's a bit like cigarettes. Low-tar filtered cigarettes probably beat unfiltered Lucky Strikes for one's health, but even cigarette-maker Altria wouldn't advertise that "the more smokers of low-tar filtered cigarettes the better."

This is hardly to say that the world's billion or so low-income people shouldn't drive. They have every right to do so, and as far and as often as anyone else. The point is that all car driving needs to converge on levels sustainable for the Earth's climate—and as soon as possible. Divided among all the world's people, this amounts to very little driving—in any vehicle—until car manufacture, operation, and disposal entail at most miniscule greenhouse emissions.

Sharing the Burden

The global impasse that has stymied real action on climate change is fundamentally the confusion of *countries* with *people* in sharing the burden. Countries aren't conscious beings. They're political entities, accidents of the history of boundary-making. People, by contrast, experience life and in doing so inevitably produce varying levels of greenhouse gas emissions.

Every human being, whether in the United States or China or Nigeria, has the same right to emit greenhouse gases as the most profligate of us do. And Americans emit many times more on average than Chinese or Nigerians do. That's why it's up to the profligate emitters—Americans among them—to cut their emissions first and to finance any emissions cuts they expect from low-emitters in other countries.

The Honda ad is a reminder of what high-emitting countries are learning too slowly: that effective global action on climate change requires convergence on very low per capita greenhouse gas emissions—or at least economics that accommodates the discrepancies. Until this basic principle of fairness is recognized and embraced by wealthy countries, progress on climate change will be incremental, in Copenhagen and beyond. And that won't be enough to save the planet, to quote Honda, "for all of us."

6

Electric Cars Make the United States More Competitive

Pew Environment Group

The Pew Environment Group is a division of the Pew Charitable Trusts, an organization of public policy think tanks. The Environment Group focuses on pragmatic, science-based global environmental protection and clean energy policies.

Electric cars will make the United States more competitive by reducing the economic and national security impact of America's dependence on oil. For example, the manufacture of electric vehicles (EVs) and the creation of charging infrastructure will create jobs. Moreover, investment in EVs and charging technology will make the United States competitive with nations such as China and South Korea, who are already making significant EV investments. In addition, EV investment will reduce the money spent and personnel deployed defending America's oil security and improve the nation's international influence. Indeed, the United States should pursue aggressive policies that stimulate EV demand and reduce obstacles to their success.

National policies that promote vehicle electrification are critical to reducing America's dependence on foreign oil, reinvigorating U.S. manufacturing and minimizing environmental impacts while enhancing the nation's competitiveness in the global clean energy economy. If the United States committed to deploying 10 million charging stations and making

25 percent of new vehicles electric by 2020, it would yield benefits that could help strengthen economic, national and environmental security far into the 21st century.

A Heavy Reliance on Oil

In the United States, 94 percent of cars, trucks, ships and planes depend on oil. In 2009, this country imported 11.7 million barrels of crude oil and refined petroleum products per day. At $100 a barrel, this amounts to sending foreign countries—some of them hostile to U.S. interests—more than $1.1 billion to meet our daily energy needs. To ensure stability in the world oil markets, American troops are deployed on oil-security missions, costing U.S. taxpayers $67 billion to $83 billion a year, according to the Rand Corp.

The United States also faces increased competition for oil from developing nations. According to the U.S. Energy Information Administration, developing nations will account for 85 percent of new energy demand through 2035. To avoid the crippling economic and security effects of dependence on a commodity that is increasingly scarce and more expensive, America's vehicle fleet must become more efficient and able to use alternative sources of fuel, such as electricity.

Manufacturing and Investment Opportunities

Manufacturing is one of the largest U.S. economic sectors, providing more than 11.6 million direct jobs. Vehicle manufacturing accounts for almost 700,000 jobs, and recent growth in this industry is contributing to the nation's economic recovery. Manufacturers are making new investments in electric vehicles (EVs) to meet consumer demand; General Motors Corp. announced that it will double production of the Chevy Volt in 2011. Underscoring the demand for electric vehicles, the first production line of the Nissan Leaf sold out six months before the vehicle went on sale. Ford Motor Co. offers an electric commercial van, the Transit Connect, and will begin selling its all-electric Focus by the end of 2011. Demand for EVs has resulted in new battery and component manufacturing facilities across the United States. The Department of Energy estimates that the United States will have the capacity to produce 40 percent of the world's advanced vehicle batteries by 2015, and other experts predict that battery manufacturing could grow to $100 billion a year by 2030.

Fuel costs for EVs are typically 2 to 3 cents a mile, whereas owners of conventional vehicles with average fuel efficiency pay more than 13 cents a mile when gasoline prices are $3 a gallon.

Investments in charging infrastructure offer significant economic opportunities as well. The U.S. market for supply and installation of residential charging points alone is expected to reach almost $1 billion by 2020. Investments made in the American Recovery and Reinvestment Act are deploying infrastructure in urban areas to collect information on how charging stations are used and will help ensure that EVs can be charged effectively and conveniently.

Though the United States has made critical initial investments in EVs and charging infrastructure, it will face intense competition for production and installation of these technologies. Overseas, China hopes to produce 500,000 EVs annually beginning in 2011 and is investing $15 billion in EV research, purchase incentives and charging stations. South Korea has also launched its Battery 2020 Project, which aims to invest $12 billion in battery technologies to become the world leader in rechargeable battery production in 10 years.

Vehicles fueled by electricity are far more efficient than conventional vehicles, sometimes achieving efficiency equivalents of 100 mpg. When these vehicles run on batteries alone, the cost of driving is significantly lower than with conventional vehicles. Fuel costs for EVs are typically 2 to 3 cents a mile, whereas owners of conventional vehicles with average fuel efficiency pay more than 13 cents a mile when gasoline prices are $3 a gallon. At these prices, an EV owner will save up to $10,000 over the vehicle's lifetime, compared with a conventional vehicle.

National Security and Environment Benefits

As noted previously, the United States spends billions of dollars a year on oil-security missions, requiring mobilization and deployment of a significant number of military personnel. Recent political instability in the Middle East has disrupted oil markets. A 2010 report by CNA's Military Advisory Board confirmed that "[o]ur dependence on foreign oil reduces our international influence, places our troops in dangerous global regions, funds nations and individuals who wish us harm and weakens our economy." The Department of Defense has aggressively sought to reduce its dependence on foreign oil, which accounts for more than 80 percent of the U.S. government's total energy consumption. The Navy, for example, aims to reduce its petroleum use in the commercial fleet by 50 percent by 2015. If the United States reduces its dependence on oil imports, the Department of Defense can meet its national security obligations at a far lower cost.

Emission Reductions

EVs emit far fewer greenhouse gases than conventional vehicles. Although power plants use various types of fuel to generate electricity, even plug-in hybrid EVs powered by older coal plants emit approximately 25 percent fewer greenhouse gases compared with conventional vehicles. Plug-in hybrids charged with electricity from zero emission power plants can achieve a 66 percent reduction in emissions. With transportation accounting for more than 31 percent of annual greenhouse gas emissions in the United States, broad adoption of EVs will dramatically lower emissions from this sector.

A Path Forward

To fully realize the benefits from large-scale adoption of EVs, national policies are needed to help stimulate demand and ensure that EVs do not encounter technical or logistical obstacles. Some of these policies include:

- Adoption of a national goal for deployment of EVs and infrastructure, including 10 million charging stations by 2020, and invest in programs to deploy new charging infrastructure in communities around the nation. Financial incentives provided to localities that develop innovative plans to accelerate deployment of EVs and charging stations will help address consumer "range anxiety"—the fear of becoming stranded too far from a charge. Continued provision of effective purchase incentives that can be realized immediately by consumers to spur sales and help manufacturers achieve economies of scale.

- A higher cap on EV purchase incentives.

- More research and development investments in vehicle technologies, especially rapid charging devices and long-lasting batteries.

7

China Not Embracing Electric Cars

Nathan Bomey

Nathan Bomey is a business reporter for the Detroit Free Press, a newspaper that serves Detroit, Michigan, a seat of the American automotive industry.

Claims that China will outpace the United States in the electric vehicle (EV) race are unfounded. In fact, Chinese consumers are as reluctant as many Americans to embrace EVs. Despite suffocating pollution in big Chinese cities and the fact that many Chinese are first-time car buyers, Chinese consumers are not buying EVs. As in the United States, EVs are more expensive and those who can afford EVs want to buy luxury, gas-powered cars. The Chinese are nevertheless committed to pursuing EV technology.

Fears that China will catapult past the U.S. in the race to put electric vehicles on the road have fizzled.

Facing the Same Obstacles

Despite choking pollution in big Chinese cities, the government faces the same obstacles as the U.S. in the push for electric vehicles [EVs]: They're still expensive, many consumers don't understand them and many drivers don't have anywhere to charge the batteries.

Although China has offered tax incentives on electric vehicles in an effort to reduce the massive air pollution problem, there are few of the vehicles on the roads.

"I think everyone would say it hasn't really taken root yet," GM China President Bob Socia said last month [April 2013] near the Shanghai auto show. "Objectives are worthy, but progress is slow."

Automakers will have to persuade Chinese consumers to give electric vehicles a try. Experts once said that Chinese consumers would embrace electric vehicles because four out of five car buyers are purchasing a vehicle for the first time. They've never had an experience with internal combustion engine cars, so they won't know what they're missing, the thinking goes.

That thinking was wrong.

Similarly, progress is slow in the U.S. The federal government offers tax credits of up to $7,500 for the purchase of an electric vehicle or semi-electric car, such as the Nissan Leaf or Chevrolet Volt. But most people are still buying conventional vehicles.

That means the door is still open for leaders to emerge in the electric vehicle space, as researchers pursue next-generation technologies amid a growing consensus that the current technology of lithium-ion batteries won't get much better or cheaper.

In 2012, the Chinese bought 12,791 hybrid and electric vehicles, according to the Chinese Association of Automobile Manufacturers.

But the real number of electric vehicles sold in China last year was actually about 3,000, when factoring out hybrids and vehicles that aren't roadworthy, such as golf carts, said Namrita Chow, a Shanghai-based analyst for IHS Automotive.

"EVs haven't taken off for a number of reasons," she said. "Consumers are not comfortable with electric vehicles."

US and Chinese EV Goals

In the U.S. in 2012, automakers sold 53,172 plug-in electric vehicles and 434,498 hybrids, representing a total market share of 3.4%, according to HybridCars.com. President Barack Obama's administration has rescinded its previous target of putting 1 million electric vehicles on the road by 2015.

The Chinese government set a goal of getting 500,000 electric vehicles on the road by 2015, with the central and provincial governments offering incentives and investing in infrastructure.

"They're going to continue to push it ... there are some pretty fundamental issues with respect to charging stations," Socia said.

Chow said the central government's EV incentives expired Dec. 31, "which means everyone is waiting" for new subsidies to be announced under China's new president, Xi Jinping.

But Yale Zhang, managing director of Automotive Foresight Shanghai, said "half a million" is not a "mandatory target" set by the government. "It takes 10 years to have this segment be more realistic," he said.

People who can afford expensive cars in China prefer luxury gasoline-powered vehicles like BMW, Audi, Mercedes-Benz and Buick.

The Impact of Vehicle Cost

In both countries, electric vehicles are more expensive than traditional vehicles. For example, the Volt, the most popular plug-in electric vehicle in the U.S. last year, starts at $40,000. Price is a big obstacle for many U.S. buyers.

"It's exactly the same here," Chow said of China. "Even with the subsidies, the cost of EVs is way higher than a traditional gasoline-powered engine vehicle."

Silicon Valley-based start-up Tesla Motors is opening dealerships in Shanghai and Beijing with high hopes for its Model S luxury electric sedan. GM sells the Chevy Volt in China in limited quantities, and Chinese automaker BYD, backed by billionaire Warren Buffett, markets its own electric vehicle.

But people who can afford expensive cars in China prefer luxury gasoline-powered vehicles like BMW, Audi, Mercedes-Benz and Buick.

"Brand image is really, really important—and if you look at some of the EV choices, they're not necessarily aligned with the high-end brand image," said Steve Merkl, president of transportation solutions for auto supplier TE Connectivity, who previously ran the company's China-based Asia business.

That's why some automakers are tinkering with their electric-vehicle strategies in China. For example, BMW and its joint venture partner, Brilliance Auto, plan to launch a new electric-vehicle brand in China called Zinoro later this year.

But some automakers announce electric vehicle plans in China for show, with few intentions of following through, Chow said.

"They want to appease the government," she said.

Still, many automakers are hoping for breakthroughs from their Chinese operations. Technology developed in China can be applied to electric vehicles throughout the world.

GM is conducting EV research with its joint venture partner, SAIC [Science Applications International Corporation], and is conducting battery cell testing, validation and chemistry research on its own at its new Advanced Technical Center in Shanghai. In a tour of the center, which finished its second phase of expansion in November, GM executives said the Shanghai facility has the same battery capabilities as the sprawling GM Technical Center in Warren.

Debbie Murphy, GM's director of China engineering, said there's "a potential" to start procuring battery cells from Chinese suppliers, too. Currently, GM gets cells from Korea-based

LG Chem and turns them into battery packs at a plant in Brownstown Township [Michigan].

"Batteries are a key focus for China, and that will enable them to get more electric vehicles here quicker," she said. "That's why we decided China was the right place to do this."

8

Selling Electric Vehicles Like Smartphones Will Make Them Appealing

Carl Pope

Carl Pope is the former executive director and chairman of the Sierra Club, an environmental advocacy organization, and coauthor, with Paul Rauber, of Strategic Ignorance: Why the Bush Administration Is Recklessly Destroying a Century of Environmental Progress.

To improve sales, manufacturers of electric vehicles should sell their products using the service-contract model used to sell smartphones. Electric cars are expensive, so to encourage people to buy them manufacturers should sell them at the same price as an equivalent gasoline model. However, buyers would also purchase a fuel contract, in which they paid an agreed upon price for the electric fuel equivalent of current gas prices for a five-year period. Using this strategy, manufacturers would recover the cost of the electric vehicle in the same way smartphone manufacturers recover the upfront cost of the phone. Increased electric car sales would in turn spur the development of better, long-range batteries and a fuelling infrastructure. To improve the market for electric cars, manufacturers should embrace the smartphone business model.

Three big barriers are slowing electric vehicles. One can be fixed by the auto industry tomorrow—and if it is, the other two will melt away as the electric vehicle sector expands.

Start with a simple but surprising fact: Right now, leasing a GM Volt for only two years costs you less than its gasoline counterpart, the Cruze. The Volt leases for $69 a month more than the Cruze, but saves $200 a month in fuel by operating most of the time on electricity. The $1800 higher down payment for leasing the Volt is paid off in 14 months—you make money for the last 10 months of your lease!

Making Electric Cars Affordable

Almost no one knows this—GM hasn't been shouting about it from the roof-tops. Clearly the company loses money leasing Volts at this price. Because most drivers don't lease, GM knows it won't, if it keeps the secret, sell more Volts at a loss than it wants to.

But the choice of a below-cost lease as a way to build the market for the Volt—along with the necessity of doing so stealthily—shows that the auto industry hasn't figured out that electric cars need to be sold differently than internal combustion engines—just as Apple had to develop new business models to sell smartphones. Imagine—and it's just as feasible as GM's current lease offer—that you could buy a Volt, or a Nissan LEAF, for the same price as its gasoline equivalent—the Cruze or the Versa. The same price! There would be a catch; to qualify, you would sign a five-year fuel contract requiring you to buy all of the electricity you needed for your car for the equivalent of $3 per gallon. You would get a better car, and guaranteed protection against future increases in the price of gas, for no additional purchase price. Your risk? Gas averages below $3.

This is how smartphones are sold. The upfront cost of the phone is recovered through a service contract—and in my model above, over five years the owner of the new electric car would pay the current sticker price of a Volt or LEAF—because they would pay a premium for the electric fuel they use.

But the car would cost less upfront than a gasoline model, and fueling the car would also cost less (unless gas averaged below $3 a gallon over the five-year period.)

Barriers to Leasing

So *Barrier One* is that the auto industry doesn't know how to sell electric cars. Electrics are smartphones, and car companies are like the old clunky AT&T monopoly—after all, they still haven't figured out how to sell them for a fixed price!

Barrier One is critical, because if GM offered a version of my fuel contract for the Volt, sales would leap, and volume would follow, and GM would make money. In turn, the auto industry would quickly solve Barriers Two and Three.

The appropriate business model [is to sell] innovative cars like innovative smartphones with a low upfront cost recovered with a fuel service contract.

Barrier Two is the slow development of a critical primary technology—batteries. The Volt and LEAF have a high sticker price—about $15,000 higher than their gas equivalents— mainly because of battery cost and performance. Full electrics don't get the range American drivers need for the same reason. (Even my fuel contract sales model for electrics requires the $7500 federal rebate to pay off the auto companies—that $7500 is about the actual economic cost premium for an electric car with gas at current US prices.)

Advanced battery companies have been suffering in the market—one, two, three, just went into bankruptcy—because the early electric cars that were their market haven't been selling fast enough. So getting sales of the Volt, LEAF and other early electrics up fast is a key to solving the battery problem.

The *final barrier* is that the necessary enabling technologies for electric cars are not in place because there has been a lack of certainty that electrification was the future. In 1910 about 1/3 of the cars on the road were electric—and steam engines were widely viewed as the future. The internal combustion engine's lock on the auto market arrived only in 1915 when Charles Kettering invented the self-starter, which neither electrics nor steam cars needed. Electric vehicles are a fundamental shift from the internal combustion drive train, and enabling technologies keyed to them have not yet been perfected. Weight is key, because energy density with electrics is lower than with gasoline—so approaches like those embodied in the XPRIZE winner Edison2's Very Light Car are incredibly important—and perhaps four to five years from maturity. Right now companies like Edison2 have a hard time raising capital because the market for weight reduction technologies—like in-wheel suspension—grows much faster in an electric car world than in one still dominated by internal combustion engines.

So there are three barriers—two of them technological—blocking the electric vehicles from dominating the auto market. But the *important barrier* is not technical at all; it is adopting the appropriate business model and selling innovative cars like innovative smartphones with a low upfront cost recovered with a fuel service contract.

9

Hybrids Are the Most Economically Viable Alternative Fuel Vehicles

Jeremy Michalek, interviewed by Megan McArdle

Jeremy Michalek is associate professor of engineering and public policy and mechanical engineering at Carnegie Mellon University, where while working with other researchers he became interested in electric vehicles and their life-cycle implications. Michalek is interviewed by Megan McArdle, who is a contributing editor at The Daily Beast.

Plug-in hybrids are currently a better alternative to gasoline-powered cars than electric vehicles (EVs). In truth, EVs currently have a limited range and long fuelling times, making them impractical for many drivers, and the cost of producing larger batteries to improve the range of EVs is currently prohibitive. Moreover, producing larger batteries creates significant carbon emissions. Indeed, many large-battery electric cars create more overall emissions than most gasoline hybrids. Thus, policies that promote plug-in hybrids are a better way to spend taxpayer money. Since EVs are not yet and may never be widespread, supporting hybrids as an incremental step is less costly than creating an expensive charging infrastructure that may never be used, and does more good for the environment.

I wrote that taxing carbon wouldn't necessarily make electric vehicles economically viable. [A couple days later] I did an interview with Professor Jeremy Michalek of Carnegie Mellon, who has done research into that very question. The interview has been lightly edited to enhance readability.

Megan: So to start with, can you tell me a bit about yourself, and how you got interested in the question of electric vehicles?

Jeremy Michalek: Sure. I'm an Associate Professor of Engineering & Public Policy and Mechanical Engineering at Carnegie Mellon University. I've been interested in vehicles since I was a kid growing up near Detroit. I became particularly interested in electric vehicles while working with other researchers at Carnegie Mellon examining their life cycle implications. The mix of issues with transportation, power generation, air emissions, fuel diversification, and policy makes it an exciting topic.

The Advantages and Disadvantages

Can you walk me through some of those issues? What are the key advantages—and disadvantages—of electric vehicles compared to gasoline-powered cars?

The key problem with "pure" electric vehicles (battery electric vehicles [BEVs]) is that they have limited range and take a long time to refuel.

Cost of batteries is the largest barrier to penetration of plug-in vehicles.

The convenient aspect is that you can refuel them from home, but then you have a problem when you want to take a longer trip with them. For example, when I visit my family in Michigan, it's a 320-mile trip, about 5 hours. If I were driving a Nissan Leaf, even at the best efficiency (and even if every rest stop had the fastest refueling capabilities) I'd have to stop at nearly every rest stop nearly every hour, to charge for a half hour. This turns my 5 hour trip into more like an 8 hour trip.

The advantage of pure electric vehicles is no gasoline consumption and no tailpipe emissions. But there are still emissions involved in producing electricity and batteries.

The plug-in hybrid electric vehicle is a nice compromise: using electricity for short trips and switching to gasoline when it's needed.

But then there's the added expense of the battery?

True. I shouldn't have said the key problem with BEVs is range and refueling time without also mentioning cost.

If the extra battery is small, the added expense is small, and there's a chance to make up that cost in fuel savings. If the extra battery is large, the added expense is large, but the additional gasoline displaced has diminishing returns. Cost of batteries is the largest barrier to penetration of plug-in vehicles.

The nice thing about small-battery plug-in hybrid electric vehicles (with gasoline backup) is that the battery is relatively small and can potentially pay for itself in fuel cost savings now or in the near future.

Evaluating Battery Cost

I get conflicting stories about whether battery cost is falling a great deal, or only slowly and incrementally improving. Do you have a sense of why it's so hard to tell whether batteries are getting cheaper and better?

There are a lot of reasons.

One is that numbers cited often compare apples and oranges. If someone quotes a kilowatt per hour (kWh) cost for batteries, one should ask whether this is referring to the cells alone, or the entire pack—which includes power electronics, packaging, cooling infrastructure, etc.

The cost also varies depending on the power requirements: smaller battery packs cost more per kWh than larger battery packs, because they need to be designed to deliver more power per cell. Some people even cite things like the costs of laptop batteries, and other batteries that are not adequate for automotive applications.

Finally, the future cost of batteries will depend on a lot of factors, such as the size of the economies of scale we get with higher production volume, how much we learn about how to manufacture batteries more efficiently, and the magnitude of technological advances that could bring costs down. Any projection made about these factors into the future will be uncertain, so I'm skeptical of anyone who offers a single point estimate for future costs.

Do you think it's plausible that we'll get to a battery cost that will make pure electric cars competitive with hybrids or old-fashioned internal combustion engines?

Yes, it's plausible, but that doesn't mean it will happen. The nice thing about small-battery plug-in hybrid electric vehicles (with gasoline backup) is that the battery is relatively small and can potentially pay for itself in fuel cost savings now or in the near future. These vehicles cost a lot less, so we can buy more of them with a given pool of money, and they are more likely to have sustainable market adoption in the near future.

Pure battery electric vehicles are far more dependent on future battery prices dropping to low levels, and we don't yet know if that will happen. Even if it does happen in the future, starting small is likely the best way to get there.

Think of it this way: If you have a 10-mile battery in a plug-in hybrid electric vehicle, then nearly every time you drive the vehicle, you use most of that 10-mile range to displace gasoline. The investment in the battery is well utilized. In contrast, if you have a 40-mile battery, for many shorter trips this investment is nothing but dead weight.

Displacing Gasoline

That's really interesting. I wouldn't have thought of it that way. That's what you mean by "diminishing returns" in terms of gasoline displacement?

Yes. The first mile worth of battery capacity added to the vehicle will displace gasoline every time you use it. The 40th mile of capacity will displace gasoline only on trips over 40 miles.

And that's one of the reasons that your research found that even if we priced the negative externalities of gasoline use—like carbon emissions—we still wouldn't end up all driving electric cars?

Yes. Carbon prices over $100 a ton are enough to dramatically change the electricity sector, yet they do little to effect electric vehicle economics. Carbon pricing would affect the price of gasoline, but it would also affect the price of electricity and batteries.

In some places, the price of electricity would presumably go up even faster than the price of gasoline, right?

When you say "even faster," what do you mean? Per mile traveled?

Electricity cost is a small portion of the overall cost of vehicle ownership, but an economy-wide carbon price will affect the cost of all goods that release carbon in their production (and use). This means they increase the price of raw battery materials at mines, the price of shipping those materials and running the factories that produce the batteries.

Is there a carbon price that would make EVs economically viable (without assuming some dramatic fall in the price of batteries)? Or is it like the Red Queen's paradox: you run faster and faster, but never get there?

Yes, but the exact price depends on a lot of factors. For example, what is the future price of gasoline and batteries? How long will batteries last before they need to be replaced? What discount rate do consumers use to weigh higher purchase cost now vs. fuel cost savings in the future? Etc.

Even under optimistic conditions ... [electric vehicles] are only marginally better than hybrids.

Given all of these uncertain factors, it's not appropriate to cite an exact carbon price, but what we do know is that very high prices (we use $140/ton as a high case in our study) do little to change the economics of plug-in vehicles.

Greenhouse gas emissions from personal transportation are significant. But they aren't the only factor that matters. Reducing oil consumption has its own benefits, and it turns out that air pollution from producing and operating vehicles causes a substantial portion of overall costs.

Looking at all of these together, electric vehicles aren't necessarily better than today's gasoline hybrids. Even under optimistic conditions (charging with zero-emissions electricity, assuming the battery lasts the life of the vehicle, etc.) they are only marginally better than hybrids.

Making Realistic Assumptions

And presumably, those optimistic assumptions aren't particularly realistic: we're not all going to be charging with our rooftop solar panels or wind turbines.

Exactly. Even if you have a solar panel on your roof, if you charge your vehicle at night (as most of us would), the electricity generated to charge that vehicle will come from coal in many regions. It's not just about the average electricity in a region—it matters which plants would turn on to meet the extra demand from your plug-in vehicle. In many regions at night, where demand is low, some coal plants turn off. If extra charging demand is added at night, coal plants may be the first to turn back on in response (because they are cheap).

So under realistic assumptions, it gets much worse: you're re-placing dirty gasoline with dirty coal power. Even if coal power is more efficient than an internal combustion engine, you just don't get big gains.

[Plug-in hybrids] offer most of the benefits of pure EVs at lower cost and with fewer infrastructure requirements.

Realistic assumptions vary from region to region (and time of day), but yes. With the average US grid mix, and including the full life cycle, electric vehicles with large battery packs can cause more overall emissions than today's gasoline hybrids. Under optimistic conditions, they offer some benefits.

When we monetize these benefits, they come out to about $1000 worth of unpriced social benefits (reduction of air emissions and gasoline consumption) over the life of the vehicle under optimistic conditions. Not enough to make up for the cost of the battery back.

On the other hand, low-range plug-in hybrids (with gasoline backup) look good. They offer most of the benefits of pure EVs at lower cost and with fewer infrastructure requirements. Hybrids don't have the barriers to consumer adoption like range limitations and the logistical challenges of parking and charging.

Hybrids do help move us down the learning curves for battery and vehicle production, helping to make pure EVs more economically competitive in the future. Pure EVs offer more gasoline savings per vehicle, but hybrids and plug-in hybrids offer more savings per dollar. If we have limited funds to spend in encouraging adoption, we should focus on the latter, not the former.

The Impact of Policy

That's a pretty important finding, and not one that you hear about very often. At least here in Washington.

We think that current plug-in vehicle subsidies are misaligned with their benefits. The policy assumes that larger batteries are significantly better. Our results suggest that bigger isn't necessarily better—on average it is worse, and in optimistic conditions larger battery plug-in vehicles are only marginally better than small battery vehicles.

We have discussed these findings on Capitol Hill.

If I may ask, what sort of reception did you get? Did you feel as if people were open to hearing that a plug-in hybrid approach was the way to go? Because most of the people I talk to here tend to get excited by the whizzy pure-electric cars like the Tesla.

[Hybrid vehicles] offer more net air emission and gasoline displacement benefits than electric vehicles with larger batteries.

Mostly quite positive. I've found generally that Congressional staffers like to have all of the information, and we've spoken to the non-partisan research groups like the Congressional Budget Office and the Congressional Research Service, who are seeking truth.

What impact that has on policy in the end is still a question. One staffer told me that the problem is if they try to change the existing policy in today's climate, we may lose it all together.

The Tesla is a fine car, by the way. But I don't see a strong case for focusing our taxpayer dollars on this type of car based on its benefits and potential to be a mass-market vehicle. Pure-electric vehicles are perfectly respectable choices for enthusiasts, as commuter vehicles, and for those who simply like them. But when it comes to spending taxpayer dollars, we should be aiming to get the largest reductions in emissions and gasoline consumption that we can.

That means focusing on efficient gasoline vehicles—including gasoline-powered hybrid vehicles—as well as low-range plug-in hybrid electric vehicles, like the Toyota Prius Plug-in Hybrid vehicle, which stores enough electricity for 12 miles of electric travel and switches to gasoline for longer trips. Our studies show that vehicles like these actually offer more net air emission and gasoline displacement benefits than electric vehicles with larger batteries, because of the emissions associated with producing the batteries, producing electricity, and carrying around the extra weight of large batteries.

Today's policies favor larger batteries: The electric vehicle tax credits established in the 2009 stimulus package give larger subsidies for larger battery packs up to $7500 per vehicle, and California's misleadingly-named "zero-emission vehicle" mandate forces automakers to build vehicles like pure electric vehicles. These policies are consuming limited resources that could achieve more good if they were deployed elsewhere. In fact, the Congressional Budget Office found that electric vehicle subsidies and mandates offer no net benefits, since the federal fuel economy standards allow automakers who sell electric vehicles to sell a corresponding number of low-efficiency vehicles resulting in no change to total fuel consumption.

A future with high gas prices, clean electricity, and cheap, long-lasting, rapidly-charged batteries would benefit pure electric vehicles. But regardless of potential futures, forcing sales of pure electric vehicles now is not the best way to get there. Rather than favoring specific technologies, we can save more gasoline and reduce more emissions at lower cost with a comprehensive focus on the end goals, including incentives that internalize the cost of pollution and oil dependency and policies that target the most cost-effective options.

Targeting Lower-Emissions Vehicles

As I understand it, the four main ways that government can target lower-emissions transportation are tax credits/subsidies, R&D assistance, building supporting infrastructure, and carbon pric-

ing. Can you talk about the right mix of those things? Do we know what the "right" mix is?

First, carbon pricing should be more general, since it's not just about carbon: It's also about gasoline and about air pollution. One of the things that surprised me in our study is the important role of air pollution. I expected it to be a minor portion of the overall social costs of vehicle production and use, but it turns out to still be quite significant. So the fourth approach is more generally to tax externalities, which could include other emissions besides carbon and could include other taxes on gasoline besides carbon taxes.

The foundation of lower-emissions transportation policy should be taxing the damages done by producing and operating vehicles at a rate equal to the damage they cause. This encourages people to drive smaller cars, drive less, or buy more fuel-efficient vehicles, but it leaves the consumers with the freedom to buy what you want (as long as you pay for the damages you cause). Revenue from such a policy could also be used to lower taxes on things we want to encourage (like employment).

The benefit of targeting a more incremental step with plug-in hybrid electric vehicles is that they cost less now, and can even pay for themselves under some conditions.

R&D is also important, since companies competing in a free market typically under-invest in research (because the benefits of their findings are too often spread among them and their competitors). Government investment in R&D is one of the few ways we could make a technology breakthrough in batteries that would make electric vehicles more affordable.

Infrastructure, in terms of public charging infrastructure, is a very expensive way of saving gasoline. We have a study out this month in *Energy Policy* estimating that workplace and retail charging infrastructure costs at least $10–20 per gallon of gasoline saved. It's cheaper to buy more batteries or cars.

Finally, tax credits and subsidies can be justified if they help us "get over the hump" into a self-sustaining future of electric vehicles that we would not be able to get over otherwise. The problem is, there is no guarantee we can get there for pure electric vehicles—many uncertain factors would have to align (cheap long-lasting batteries, expensive gasoline, etc.).

The benefit of targeting a more incremental step with plug-in hybrid electric vehicles is that they cost less now, and can even pay for themselves under some conditions. Studies have shown they are preferred by consumers to pure EVs, they provide more environmental good on average in the near to medium term, and they avoid the need to invest in costly infrastructure that will be mothballed if EVs don't take off. (That infrastructure, by the way, comes with assorted vandalism, obsolescence, and parking logistics issues). And they leave open the option to move to either pure EVs or another technology in the future, if, say, someone comes up with a platinum-free fuel cell that makes fuel cells more competitive.

I should have named a fifth option: financing. The famous (infamous?) loan program that funded Solyndra was supposed to help companies cross that chasm to a viable product. Do you have any thoughts on whether this is necessary? Helpful?

My main comment on financing firms with innovative energy technologies is that we need to be willing to accept some level of failure. If there is no failure, then we're not taking enough risk.

10

The Government Should Subsidize Electric Cars

Nick Chambers

Nick Chambers is a car enthusiast and electric vehicle advocate who writes for The New York Times, Motor Trend, Scientific American, Popular Mechanics, *and* The Daily Green, *as well as the websites AutoTrader.com, HybridCars.com, and Gas 2.0. He was one of the first five Americans to test drive a preproduction Nissan LEAF in Japan and is an advocate of bringing electric vehicle infrastructure to rural Washington State.*

Arguments against electric car subsidies are flawed. Electric vehicles (EVs) are significantly more energy efficient than gasoline-powered cars. Moreover, claims that subsidies are a tax break for the rich ignore the fact that the subsidy and fuel-saving costs reduce the vehicle's overall cost, making EVs practical for the average American. The reason that sales of EVs are down is due largely to media misinformation about EVs. In truth, that EV haters oppose government support of industry of any kind is hypocritical, as oil drilling and electrical and highway infrastructure require government support. Electric cars can reduce fuel costs, oil pollution, and fossil fuel dependence and thus deserve government support.

After more than a decade of uninformed electric car [EV] bashing from certain segments of the population—with the last two years especially seeing an incredible spike as EVs have curiously become a political pawn piece—it's not surprising that there is a veritable smorgasbord of bad will towards the otherwise innocuous vehicles. To listen to some of the punditry talk, supporting electric cars is the equivalent of throwing your mother overboard on a cruise vacation.

A Misplaced Assault

But I wonder if those same EV-hating pundits would have pulled out the unwavering ideological argument that supporting any kind of industry with government money is anti-American and will turn your babies into helpless, socialist wards of the state back when the government poured money into our fuel and highway system? Would they go back and say that tax breaks to help oil companies drill more were a bad idea? Would they argue that government funding of the electrical grid, nuclear powerplants or any of the innumerable technologies that wouldn't exist today without government programs to support their development was the wrong decision?

There aren't many EVs (yet) so of course their impact is small. That's why it's important to encourage more of them onto the road.

Clearly EV-hating extremists aren't new news, so why is this an issue again? As PluginCars.com readers likely know by now, with the New Year [2012] a few tax credits for EVs expired: namely the 30% Federal Tax credit for the installation of a charging station. Along with this came news of a new Republican-led assault on the existing $7,500 federal tax credit towards the purchase of an EV. [As of November 2013, Congress has not chosen to eliminate this tax credit.]

And then, sensing an opportunity, over the weekend the *Washington Post* published an editorial that basically said EVs aren't ready for prime time and that all tax credits for them should be taken away, warning that "Backers of the charger tax credit may lobby Congress to renew it when lawmakers tackle the payroll tax extension issue again in the new year. We hope that Congress says no."

Half Truths and Lies

The Washington Post editorial has made the typical mistakes and assumptions that so many influenced by the propaganda machine have started to take for fact when really they are, at best, half truths or, at worst, blatant lies:

"As a means of reducing carbon emissions, electric cars and plug-in hybrid electrics are no more cost-effective than ethanol."

This claim is bogus. Electric cars are about five times more efficient (depending on what study you use) at converting energy into movement than a combustion engine of any type, whether it runs gas, diesel or ethanol. In fact, the simple act of making a gallon of gas takes just as much energy as it does to drive an electric car 40 miles. So not only is there 40 miles of energy in that gallon, it takes roughly 2 more gallons to drive the same distance as an electric car on the energy it took just creating those two gallons of gas. I suspect this argument has to do with numbers of vehicles on the road. There aren't many EVs (yet) so of course their impact is small. That's why it's important to encourage more of them onto the road (with subsidies, policies, etc.).

"Only upper-income consumers can afford to buy an electric vehicle; so the charger subsidy is a giveaway to the well-to-do."

New technology is always more expensive initially. And, while it's true that the base price of an EV is currently more expensive than that of a combustion car, the difference is not so large that only the "well-to-do" can afford them. It's about comparing apples to apples. Take the gas-powered Ford Focus; it's about the same size as the LEAF. A base Ford Focus can be bought for less than $20K, but when you add in all the equipment that makes it comparable to a LEAF it will cost you

$26K. A LEAF can be bought for $35K. Factor in the $7,500 federal tax credit and the cost effectively comes down to $27.5K; a difference of $1,500, which will more than be made up for in fuel savings over 5 years. Also, the LEAF can be leased for around $380 per month with a $2,500 down payment. That is not "well-to-do" pricing, that is middle class pricing (or used to be before a free market gone wild ruined our economy—thanks largely to the uncharacteristically unconservative policies of the so-called modern conservative).

Circular Reasoning and False Narratives

"Get rid of the $7,500 tax credit too."

The editorial goes on to say they feel similarly about the $7,500 tax credit, but that reasoning is circular. If the writers mean, as they imply, that the tax credit would be better if it was for "average Americans," then the $7,500 is what is leveling the playing field and making the technology affordable for average Americans. Of course if you take the $7,500 away then you start making the cars inaccessible to average Americans so the writers' case gets stronger. It's self-fulfilling prophecy.

"Given the price of eligible models, like the $100,000 Fisker Karma, that rationale sounds an awful lot like trickle-down economics."

The EV is an easy target for bad marketing—and the effect is a completely twisted consumer impression of what they are and what they can do.

Only a thousand of the Karmas will be sold this year if they're lucky, and a $7,500 tax credit on a $100,000 car is meaningless to those buying it. Compared to expected sales of about 50,000 to 100,000 of all the other plug-ins that are consumer priced in 2011, the amount of tax credit going to the Karma is negligible. The only reason the Karma is brought up is to further a false narrative. It's a cheap shot that has no bearing on presenting a successful argument.

"Sales of electric vehicles were disappointing in 2011, with the Volt coming in below the 10,000 units forecast."

Firstly, the writers ignore that the Leaf hit its sales target of 10,000 units. Secondly, it's no surprise that sales of EVs were slower than expected in 2011. Given the amount of misinformation being strewn about by the majority of uneducated media, the picture being painted of EVs is that they are stupid, suck money out of the government, re-distribute wealth, destroy the free market, are anti-American, don't protect your freedom, are more polluting than gas cars, and will actually cost you more in the long run—not to mention you're a sissy if you drive one. All of which are unequivocally and provably wrong.

The reality of our sad situation is that success of anything is tied into marketing, and the EV is an easy target for bad marketing—and the effect is a completely twisted consumer impression of what they are and what they can do. It's no wonder they aren't selling more. It's another self-fulfilling prophecy.

A Hypocritical Mantra

"The ethanol credit was on the books for 30 years before it finally died. Let's hope Congress can start unwinding the federal government's bad investment in electric vehicles faster than that."

The general insinuation throughout the editorial is that the government has no right meddling with the free market, a mantra that the right wing often espouses with increasing aggressiveness these days. Yet it's a hypocritical one. The modern car didn't come into being simply because some companies struggled on their own without government support. Highways, bridges, and fuel stations were all paid for (at least partially) with government funds. Our electricity infrastructure was also paid for in the same way.

The U.S. government has a solid and successful tradition of propping up new technologies for a few decades before they become as second nature as having a fridge or flipping a switch. To claim otherwise is sheer stupidity. The electric car can kill several birds with one stone: pollution, oil dependence, national security, and fuel price shock. It is a great solution to our needs as a nation and, with the right support, is the best thing we can do to help our nation's transportation needs in the future. Without that support it will never come, but then again, neither would have our nation's electricity grid or system of highways. We'd clearly be in a better position today without those, right?

11

The Government Should Not Subsidize Electric Cars

Mark J. Perry

Mark J. Perry, professor of economics and finance at the University of Michigan, is a scholar at the American Enterprise Institute, a conservative think tank.

Subsidies for electric cars are a boondoggle that Americans can do without. Such subsidies distort demand and discourage development of better alternative fuel vehicles. Nevertheless, fearing ever-rising foreign oil imports, the Obama administration thought electric cars and plug-in hybrids were necessary to offset rising fuel costs. In fact, oil imports are down and American refineries have plenty of fuel, making subsidies unwarranted. Americans are not buying electric cars because they are too expensive. Instead, many American consumers buy cheaper, fuel efficient, gasoline-powered vehicles. If the electric car was a viable commodity, it would not need government support. Indeed, these subsidies contradict the free market principles that form the core of the nation's economy.

For the first time in a few years, electric cars are mostly an afterthought at the auto show in Detroit.

To be sure, electric cars and hybrid electric models are on the show floor and still being promoted at various intensity levels by Detroit's automakers as well as Japanese companies and upstarts building—but not selling many—high-priced, electric sports cars. But the niche vehicles are not as prominent this year [2012] as in past years.

That's a good thing.

Distorting Demand

Electric vehicles aren't the answer to curbing America's dependence on foreign oil or putting a dent in climate change.

That is evidenced by lackluster sales of the vehicles that came propped up by generous taxpayer subsidies and corporate purchases that distort the actual demand by everyday consumers.

General Motors Co., for example, sold 7,671 Volts, far fewer than its goal of 10,000 and the company didn't break down how many of those sales were to showroom shoppers or to government or corporate fleets. Nissan Motor Co., another big promoter of electric vehicles, sold 9,674 all-electric Leafs, according to Autodata Corp.

By now, you'd think that the government would have stopped forcing American taxpayers to subsidize the electric car. It really never should have picked one automotive technology over another in the first place.

Subsidizing the electric car has been a devil's bargain, making the development of other alternative technologies such as conventional hybrids and advanced gasoline engines all the more difficult.

Though it's certainly the case that electric cars and trucks are part of our automotive future, taxpayer subsidies for EVs should be phased out as an unneeded cost at a time of enormous federal budget deficits. The national debt has surpassed $15 trillion.

There seems little doubt that the Obama administration's prime justification for subsidizing electric cars and plug-in hybrids—the fear that U.S. oil imports would keep rising—was way off base.

Oil imports were down to a 16-year low of 45.4 percent of domestic consumption in 2011, from a high of 60.3 percent in 2005.

And American refineries are so flush with gasoline, diesel oil and other petroleum products that the U.S. became a net exporter of fuel last year for the first time since 1949.

The environmental and economic benefits of electric cars are likely to be relatively modest.

Subsidies for electric cars were also supposed to lower their operating costs so that popularity of the vehicles could reduce global warming. President Barack Obama predicted that 1 million electric cars would be on the road by 2015.

Sales Lagging Badly

But electric car sales are lagging. Costs have not dropped to become competitive with gasoline-powered vehicles and the environmental and economic benefits of electric cars are likely to be relatively modest.

And, everyone knows that electric cars are too expensive.

The average American can't afford an electric car, no matter what the model is. Even with a federal tax credit of up to $7,500, the $40,000-plus price of a Chevy Volt is about double that of a comparable gasoline model.

That's not to suggest that consumers don't care about fuel efficiency. They do. GM sold 231,732 Chevy Cruzes in 2011. The compact car gets close to 40 miles per gallon and the Eco version gets 42 mpg on the highway, according to the Department of Energy. It also costs far less at a starting price of about $17,000.

Revealingly, most of the Volts are sold in California, where buyers receive an extra tax credit of $1,500 and an additional bonus—electric cars can drive in HOV lanes on California's clogged freeways.

It is highly unlikely that GM will double or triple those sales this year. In December, GM CEO Dan Akerson said the company planned to sell 45,000 Volt's this year.

Let the Market Decide

The case for subsidizing electric cars was questionable from the start and is now a boondoggle.

Like many green initiatives promoted by the government and paid for by the American taxpayers, the electric car is more politically than performance or economically driven. Its subsidies and the government-imposed green energy mandates are contrary to the free market principles that undergird our economy.

What emerges most forcefully from experience with the electric car is that subsidies are a waste of taxpayer money. Although the government has provided plenty of help for electric vehicles, there remain major barriers in technology, cost and performance.

As battery technology improves and charging stations proliferate, we will eventually move to an electric-car future.

But the outcome of EV development needs to be like that of the internal combustion engines: the government doesn't have to subsidize regular cars because long ago, it became worthwhile for companies to do it themselves with rebates, discount pricing, and other promotions.

Private businesses will fund new technologies when there is a reasonable chance of commercial success. The private sector is entirely capable of developing EVs and other new automotive technologies without the need for subsidies.

When a new technology is economically viable, then government support is not needed. But if a technology isn't capable of surviving on its own, there's no amount of taxpayer support that will make it so.

It's time to pull the plug on politically motivated taxpayer subsidies for electric cars and see if they can survive on their own in the marketplace.

12

A Mileage Tax to Replenish Highway Revenue Is Fair

Gerald Bastarache

Gerald Bastarache is the former director of communications at the Highway Users Federation and the Intelligent Transportation Society of America and writes for the Janesville Gazette, *a Wisconsin daily newspaper.*

The gasoline tax is no longer producing enough revenue to build and maintain the roads on which Americans drive. Indeed, the current Highway Trust Fund brings in $32 billion a year when highway needs require nearly $100 billion annually. However, simply increasing the gasoline tax is unfair, as the driver of a low mpg hybrid vehicle pays less than someone who drives a 20 mpg pickup truck the same distance. A more equitable way to collect highway revenue is to tax the number of miles that drivers travel. As vehicles reduce fuel use, a vehicle mileage tax will help close the highway funding gap more equitably.

The richest nation on Earth can't pay for the roads it needs anymore. The way the U.S. government collects the money it needs for roads—through a federal tax on motor fuel—is outdated and badly needs modernization to adapt to drastically changing circumstances.

The Highway Trust Fund

In 1956, Congress came up with a "pay-as-you-go" method to fund the Interstate Highway System. Instead of floating bonds, the Federal Highway Trust Fund was created and mainly supported by federal taxes on motor fuel, then 3 cents per gallon.

The Trust Fund's guiding principle was fairness—the more you used the highways, the more you paid for them. But even though the federal motor fuel tax is now 18.4 cents per gallon, the Trust Fund is going broke.

Better fuel economy, reduced gasoline use and highway travel, and rising construction costs have caused the Highway Trust Fund to run out of money at a time when a first-class highway system is badly needed to help pull our economy out of recession.

To look into this problem, Congress created a 15-member National Surface Transportation Infrastructure Financing Commission to investigate options and recommend a course of action.

The numbers tell the tale: long-term federal highway revenues are estimated to bring in only $32-billion a year, while highway needs total almost $100-billion a year. Meanwhile, real highway spending per mile has fallen by nearly half since the Trust Fund was established.

The goal of the mileage tax is still to collect the funds we need for good highways through user fees, but in a more logical way than we do now.

The Commission's unanimous report, released in late February [2009], calls for a 10 cents per gallon boost in the federal gasoline tax—which equals one-half cent per mile—followed by a gradual shift from our current reliance on motor fuel taxes toward a fee on actual miles driven.

To measure these miles, the Commission calls for "in-vehicle or after market Global Positioning System (GPS) devices" that would track the way we drive. The per-mile charge would depend on whether the driving is on crowded urban freeways during rush hour (higher charge) or lightly traveled rural roads (lower charge).

The goal of the mileage tax is still to collect the funds we need for good highways through user fees, but in a more logical way than we do now.

The report says the amount charged for cars could range from 0.9 cents per mile to match current Trust Fund revenues, or go up to 2.3 cents per mile to "maintain and improve" the annual investment level.

Achieving Fairness

The levels of taxation require careful calibration to ensure fairness. But compared to the current system, fairness should be relatively easy to achieve.

What's fair now about charging a driver who can afford a new 40 mpg hybrid less to use the highways than a construction worker who drives a 20 mpg pickup?

"The gas tax isn't going to fill the bill," says Congressman Peter Defazio, D-Ore., a member of the House Transportation & Infrastructure Committee.

So in a pilot program, Oregon has installed GPS monitoring devices in 300 vehicles equipped with in-vehicle transponders that calculate the mileage tax owed.

Drivers in Portland continue to pay the tax at the pump, just as they have in the past. Other states, plus the Netherlands and Denmark, are considering mileage taxes.

Privacy is sometimes cited as a concern, but privacy is protected when the data is kept within the vehicle. The many GPS tracking devices already in today's vehicles, such as On-Star, E-ZPass and LoJack, are effective without compromising privacy.

Simply raising the fuel tax would be a temporary band-aid on a hemorrhaging Highway Trust Fund. As more fuel-efficient and hybrid vehicles require less motor fuel, the funding gap will only grow. And as we modernize our vehicles and reduce our motor fuel use, it's time to let the vehicle mileage tax play its role in our highway funding.

13

A Mileage Tax to Replenish Highway Revenue Is Unfair

Ethan Epstein

Ethan Epstein is an editorial assistant for the Weekly Standard, *a conservative newsmagazine.*

Replacing the gasoline tax with a vehicle mileage tax is not the solution to dwindling and much needed highway funds. Devices installed in vehicles that monitor miles driven raise privacy concerns and will require frequent and costly inspections. Strangely, the tax, supported by green policy makers, also seems to contradict the green movement's goal of rewarding those who drive cars that pollute less. In truth, dwindling funds meant for the construction and maintenance of highways are the result of their diversion to green programs such as pedestrian and bicycle paths, scenic easements, and transportation museums. The solution is to assess the current allocation of funds not a vehicle mileage tax that punishes people for driving.

Give the environmental movement credit: When it comes to reducing vehicle emissions, it has won a stupendous victory. Since 1975, when the first federal mileage per gallon standards were introduced, the average mpg for American-driven cars has zoomed from less than 15 to nearly 35. Ever-more stringent emission standards from Washington, growing environmentalist sentiment among the general public, and rising gas prices have all played a part in this phenomenon. So has the bevy of tax subsidies that the federal government offers for buying hybrids and other low-emission vehicles. Federal and state gas taxes, too, have been a potent force in encouraging drivers to switch to more fuel-efficient cars; at a rate of 18.4 cents a gallon, any driver can greatly reduce his annual federal tax bill by simply buying less fuel.

But now the green movement's hard-won gains against emissions are bumping up against another of its passions: tax revenues. Because more and more Americans have switched to less fuel-hungry cars (and because some Americans have dropped driving altogether), gas tax receipts have fallen precipitously. It's a "problem" created directly by the success of environmentalist goals.

Replacing the Gas Tax

Enter the prickly, greener-than-thou Representative Earl Blumenauer, a Democrat from Oregon, who wants to require the Treasury Department to "study" ways to replace the gas tax with a vehicle-miles traveled (VMT) tax.

The most striking thing about the VMT tax is that it appears in direct conflict with green goals.

Blumenauer—who fulfills the *Portlandia*[1] stereotype by wearing an unwieldy bicycle pin on his lapel—has long been a proponent of a VMT tax. Claiming that "it is time to get creative and find smart ways to rebuild and renew America's deteriorating infrastructure," he introduced a bill in December [2012] that would have forced the Treasury Department to "establish a pilot program to study alternatives to the current system of taxing motor vehicle fuels." The bill as drafted only

1. *Portlandia* is a satirical sketch comedy television series set and filmed in and near Portland, Oregon. The stereotype to which the author refers is, however, subject to vigorous debate. Nevertheless, in the context of the viewpoint and the author's views, he is arguably suggesting that the stereotype includes those who support a sustainable, environmentally friendly ethic for which some Oregonians are known.

mentions one "alternative": a tax "based on the number of miles driven." (The choice of having the Treasury Department study the VMT tax rather than the Department of Transportation is a shrewd one, by the way, because last year the House voted to ban the DOT from studying a VMT.)

Blumenauer's bill died in committee last month. According to his spokesman Patrick Malone, however, Blumenauer plans on reintroducing the bill in the next Congress. It's an idea that's gaining momentum. President Obama claims to oppose the VMT tax, though his transportation secretary, Ray LaHood, has said it's a proposal that "should be looked at." Several European countries are planning to implement VMT taxes in the coming decade.

Conflicting with Green Goals

Perhaps the most striking thing about the VMT tax is that it appears in direct conflict with green goals. If a Prius is suddenly taxed at the same rate as a Ford Expedition, after all, the government has removed a powerful incentive for driving cars that pollute less. Some VMT tax supporters say it "could" be structured so that less-efficient vehicles are taxed more heavily. But isn't this precisely what the gas tax accomplishes? Why switch to a complicated new system only to maintain the same fundamental structure? It's also simply not true that all cars are equally culpable in wearing down the roads; numerous studies have shown that heavy trucks cause the vast majority of damage to roads and highways.

There's an obvious privacy issue, too. Because odometers are relatively easily tampered with (and besides, using odometers to gauge miles driven would require the government to engage in frequent and costly car mileage inspections), cars would almost certainly need to be outfitted with some form of government tracking device. Blumenauer waves these concerns aside by saying that the VMT tax can be administered in a way that "protects personal privacy." Tellingly, he provides no details as to how. A VMT tax pilot program involving about 50 drivers in Blumenauer's home state of Oregon that's been in effect since 2006 isn't encouraging. According to *Governing* magazine, "That study involved using GPS devices to collect data on the number of miles traveled by each motorist, transferring the data to gas stations, and levying the appropriate fee when drivers filled their tanks."

A VMT tax, fundamentally, is a punishment for driving, regardless of how many emissions your car spews—and even if it doesn't spew any at all!

The Impact of Green Mission Creep

Rep. Blumenauer and other VMT tax proponents are right about one thing: Highway maintenance is suffering and the highway trust fund is dwindling. The American Society of Civil Engineers has given American infrastructure a grade of D. Over the past four years, Congress has transferred nearly $50 billion from the general fund to the highway trust fund just to shore it up. But this sorry state of affairs isn't only a result of falling gas tax revenues; the highway trust fund is also suffering from some serious mission creep.

A recent GAO study reported that between 2004 and 2008, some $78 billion from the highway trust fund was used for "purposes other than construction and maintenance of highways and bridges." A 2009 report prepared by the offices of Senators Tom Coburn and John McCain found that "Congress raids the highway trust fund for pet projects while bridges and roads crumble." For example, states must now spend a certain percentage of their highway trust funds on "transportation enhancement" projects. Eligible "transportation enhancement" categories include the "provision of pedestrian and bicycle facilities," the "acquisition of scenic or historic easement and sites," and the "establishment of transportation museums." In a development to warm the cockles of Rep.

Blumenauer's heart, between 2004 and 2008, $2 billion from the highway trust fund was spent on 5,500 projects for pedestrians and bicycles. Yet again, the dwindling of the highway trust fund—a problem that only a VMT tax can fix!—is a direct result of policies that Blumenauer and his green allies support.

Novelist J. G. Ballard once wrote that the personal car "enshrines a basically old-fashioned idea: freedom." In a way, critics of the contemporary greens owe Blumenauer a debt of gratitude. A VMT tax, fundamentally, is a punishment for driving, regardless of how many emissions your car spews— and even if it doesn't spew any at all! By decoupling the hatred for cars from the justifiable hatred of pollution, Blumenauer has confirmed what many critics have long suspected about some of the most zealous greens: It's not just that they love the planet. They're suspicious of freedom, too.

Organizations to Contact

The editors have compiled the following list of organizations concerned with the issues debated in this book. The descriptions are derived from materials provided by the organizations. All have publications or information available for interested readers. The list was compiled on the date of publication of the present volume; names, addresses, phone and fax numbers, and e-mail and Internet addresses may change. Be aware that many organizations take several weeks or longer to respond to inquiries, so allow as much time as possible.

American Council for an Energy-Efficient Economy (ACEEE)
529 14th St. NW, Suite 600, Washington, DC 20045-1000
(202) 507-4000 • fax: (202) 429-2248
website: www.aceee.org

Founded in 1980, the American Council for an Energy-Efficient Economy (ACEEE) actively participates in the energy debate, developing policy recommendations and documenting how energy efficiency measures can reduce energy use, air pollutants, and greenhouse gas emissions while benefiting the economy. On its website the Council publishes research reports, including *Plug-in Electric Vehicles: Challenges and Opportunities* and *Gearing Up: Smart Standards Create Good Jobs Building Cleaner Cars.*

American Petroleum Institute (API)
220 L St. NW, Washington, DC 20005-4070
(202) 682-8000
website: www.api.org

The American Petroleum Institute (API) is a trade association that represents America's oil and natural gas industry. Its mission is to influence public policy in support of a strong, viable US oil and natural gas industry. The Institute believes that oil and natural gas are essential to meet the energy needs of consumers and maintain a strong American economy. On its website the Institute provides fact sheets, articles, testimony, and reports on issues related to exploration, production, and refining of oil and natural gas, including "Renewable Fuel Standard Facts" and the report *Energizing America.*

Cato Institute

1000 Massachusetts Ave. NW, Washington, DC   20001-5403
(202) 842-0200 • fax: (202) 842-3490
website: www.cato.org

The Cato Institute is a libertarian public policy research foundation that promotes policies based on individual liberty, limited government, free markets, and peaceful international relations. Cato analysts believe that the market should determine what Americans drive. Cato fellows assert that federal subsides of hybrid and electric cars stifle innovation. The Institute publishes numerous reports and periodicals, including *Policy Analysis* and *Cato Policy Review.* Articles on hybrid and electric cars can be found on the website's searchable database, including "Stifling Innovation with Subsidies" and "The EPA's Odd View of 'Consumer Choice.'"

The Electric Generation

701 Pennsylvania Ave. NW, Washington, DC   20004-2696
(202) 508-5088
website: http://theelectricgeneration.org

The Electric Generation is a campaign supported by the Edison Electric Institute (EEI) that represents the electric utility industry's commitment to the widespread adoption of electricity as a transportation fuel. The voices of the organization are actual owners and drivers of electric vehicles and people who are passionate about driving electric cars. On its website the organization provides information on the history of electric cars as well as articles on driving and fueling electric cars. On its Current Thinking link, the organization provides articles on electric vehicles, including "An Educated Consumer Is Our Best Consumer" and "Two-Way Street: Electric Cars of the Future Could Give Power Back to the Grid."

Electric Power Research Institute (EPRI)

3420 Hillview Ave., Palo Alto, CA   94304
(800) 313-3774
e-mail: askepri@apri.com
website: www.epri.com

The Electric Power Research Institute (EPRI) is an independent nonprofit organization dedicated to researching and improving electricity generation, delivery, and use. Specific issues tackled by the Institute's researchers include reliability, efficiency, health, safety, the environment, and electric transportation. The Electric Transportation program at EPRI conducts research and development of vehicle and infrastructure technologies that enable the use of electricity as a transportation fuel. The program has played a leading role in the development of plug-in electric vehicle technologies. Publications on electric transportation can be found on the EPRI website, including the report *Total Cost of Ownership Model for Current Plug-in Electric Vehicles.*

Electrification Coalition

1111 19th St. NW, Suite 406, Washington, DC   20036
(202) 448-9300 • fax: (202) 461-2379
e-mail: Info@ElectrificationCoalition.org
website: http://electrificationcoalition.org

The Electrification Coalition is a nonprofit group of business leaders committed to promoting policies and actions that facilitate the deployment of electric vehicles. The coalition believes that oil dependence threatens the nation's economic, environmental, and national security. Thus it supports policies that encourage manufacture of electric car batteries and vehicles at a scale to bring prices down, the construction of charging infrastructure, and promotion of consumer acceptance. On its website the Coalition publishes fact sheets, articles, and reports, including the articles "The Electric Drive Bellwether?" and "The Need for Transferable Tax Credits" and the reports *Electrification Roadmap* and *State of the Plug-in Electric Vehicle Market.*

Institute of Electrical and Electronics Engineers (IEEE)
2001 L St. NW, Suite 700, Washington, DC   20036-4910
(202) 785-0017 • fax: (202) 785-0835
e-mail: ieeeusa@ieee.org
website: www.ieee.org

The Institute of Electrical and Electronics Engineers (IEEE) is a professional association of individuals involved in technology-related fields with the goal of advancing technology to improve the lives of humans around the world. The IEEE Why Electric Cars Are Our Future site is dedicated to prompting adoption of electric cars and the grid to fuel them. The web link publishes news, articles, and commentary, including "Why Electric Cars Are Our Future" and "New Batteries Please."

Pew Charitable Trusts
901 E St. NW, Washington, DC   20004-2008
(202) 552-2000 • fax: (202) 552-2299
website: www.pewtrusts.org

Funded by charitable funds established by two sons and two daughters of Sun Oil Company founder Joseph N. Pew and his wife, Mary Anderson Pew, the Pew Charitable Trusts studies and promotes nonpartisan solutions for national and global public policy problems. The Pew Environment Group seeks to protect ocean and land habitats and advocates for a clean energy economy. Its website, www.pewenvironment.org, publishes news, articles, and research, including "Gas Price Conundrum: Think Outside the Barrel" and "Reducing Oil Dependence Through Transportation Innovation."

Plug In America
2370 Market St., Suite 419, San Francisco, CA   94114
(415) 323-3329
website: www.pluginamerica.org

Plug In America is a coalition of electric vehicle (EV) owners and advocates who promote the shift to plug-in vehicles powered by clean, affordable, domestic electricity to reduce our nation's dependence on petroleum and improve the global environment. On its website the organization publishes stories from EV owners, and Plug In America bloggers explore the latest technology. The website also provides links to podcasts, videos, and other organizations that support EVs.

Union of Concerned Scientists (UCS)

Two Brattle Square, Cambridge, MA 02238
(617) 547-5552 • fax: (617) 864-9405
website: www.ucsusa.org

Founded by scientists and students at Massachusetts Institute of Technology (MIT) in 1969, the Union of Concerned Scientists (UCS) is the leading science-based nonprofit working for a healthy environment and a safer world. UCS utilizes independent scientific research and citizen action "to develop innovative, practical solutions and to secure responsible changes in government policy, corporate practices, and consumer choices." UCS publishes in-depth reports such as *State of Charge: Electric Vehicles* and *Fueling a Better Future: The Many Benefits of "Half the Oil."*

US Department of Energy (DOE) Energy Efficiency & Renewable Energy Alternative Fuels Data Center

1000 Independence Ave. SW, Washington, DC 20585
(202) 586-5000 • fax: (202) 586-4403
e-mail: The.Secretary@hq.doe.gov
website: www.energy.gov

The Department of Energy (DOE) is the US government agency charged with helping maintain American security and prosperity by finding innovative ways to tackle the country's energy, environmental, and nuclear challenges. In order to fulfill this mission, the DOE seeks to establish the United States as a leader in clean energy technology development and implementation, foster scientific research and innovation, ensure nuclear safety and security, and provide the guidelines and planning necessary to achieve these goals. The DOE has an entire website dedicated to alternative fuel vehicles and the laws and policies that impact their use. The website publishes articles on all-electric, plug-in hybrid, and hybrid electric vehicles, including the reports *Plug-in Electric Vehicles: Challenges and Opportunities* and *Overcoming Barriers to Electric-Vehicle Deployment.*

Bibliography

Books

Curtis D. Anderson and Judy Anderson	*Electric and Hybrid Cars: A History.* Jefferson, NC: McFarland & Company, 2005.
Robert U. Ayres and Edward H. Ayers	*Crossing the Energy Divide: Moving from Fossil Fuel Dependence to a Clean-Energy Future.* Upper Saddle River, NJ: Wharton School, 2009.
James Billmaier	*JOLT! The Impending Dominance of the Electric Car and Why America Must Take Charge.* Charleston, SC: Advantage Media Group, 2010.
Seth Fletcher	*Bottled Lightning: Superbatteries, Electric Cars, and the New Lithium Economy.* New York: Hill and Wang, 2011.
Allen E. Fuhs	*Hybrid Vehicles and the Future of Personal Transportation.* Boca Raton, FL: CRC Press, 2009.
Laurance R. Geri and David E. McNabb	*Energy Policy in the U.S.: Politics, Challenges, and Prospects for Change.* Boca Raton, FL: CRC Press, 2011.
Eric J. Jeffs	*Greener Energy Systems: Energy Production Technologies with Minimum Environmental Impact.* Boca Raton, FL: CRC Press, 2012.

Anne Korin and Gal Luft	*Turning Oil into Salt: Energy Independence Through Fuel Choice.* Charleston, SC: Book Surge, 2009.
Leonardo Maugeri	*Beyond the Age of Oil: The Myths, Realities, and Future of Fossil Fuels and Their Alternatives.* Westport, CT: Praeger, 2010.
Jerry McNerney	*Clean Energy Nation: Freeing America from the Tyranny of Fossil Fuels.* New York: AMACOM, 2011.
Jim Motavalli	*High Voltage: The Fast Track to Plug In the Auto Industry.* Emmaus, PA: Rodale Books, 2011.
David Owen	*The Conundrum: How Scientific Innovation, Increased Efficiency, and Good Intentions Can Make Our Energy and Climate Problems Worse.* New York: Riverhead Books, 2012.
Gianfranco Pistoia, ed.	*Electric and Hybrid Vehicles: Power Sources, Models, Sustainability, Infrastructure and the Market.* Boston: Elsevier, 2010.
Daniel Yergin	*The Quest: Energy, Security, and the Remaking of the Modern World.* New York: Penguin, 2012.

Periodicals and Internet Sources

Don Anair and Amine Mahmassani	"State of Charge: Electric Vehicles' Global Warming Emissions and the Fuel-Cost Savings Across the United States," Union of Concerned Scientists, June 2012. www.ucsusa .org.
Max Baumhefner and Cecilia Springer	"Electric Cars Are Cleaner Today and Will Only Get Cleaner Tomorrow," *Switchboard*, August 5, 2013. http:// switchboard.nrdc.org.
Bradley Berman	"Electric, if Not Electrifying: Cars for Short-Range Commutes," *New York Times*, June 12, 2011.
Allen Best	"Plugging In: Many Benefits of Electric Cars Justify Subsidies for Public Charging Infrastructure in Colorado," *Denver Post*, August 11, 2013.
Raven Clabough	"States Propose Fees on Hybrids to Cover Gas Tax Losses," *New American*, June 10, 2013.
Mike Colias	"Decoding the Volt's Price Cut: Are EVs Doomed or Going Mainstream?," *Automotive News*, Augusts 12, 2013.
Phyllis Cuttino	"Electric Vehicles Strengthen US Competitiveness," *Huffington Post*, November 7, 2012. www .huffingtonpost.com.

Jerry Hirsch	"Hybrid vs. Wallet; Is Paying More for the Gas-Electric Cars Worth it? Weigh These Factors," *Los Angeles Times*, June 10, 2012.
Michael E. Kraft	"High-Mileage Hybrids Have Huge Payoff," Phys.org, June 20, 2013. http://phys.org.
Bjorn Lomborg	"Why the Electric Car Failed, Again; Expensive and Unwieldy, These Vehicles Create More Pollution than They Prevent," *National Post*, April 22, 2013.
Jan Lundberg	"Sierra Club's Electric Cars: Is It Time for More Technology or Culture Change," Culture Change, April 13, 2012. www.culturechange.org.
John Montgomery	"Electric and Gas Cars Not an Either-or Proposition," *Hutchinson News* (KS), August 29, 2010.
Jim Motavalli	"The Road Ahead for Gasoline-Free Cars," *The Futurist*, March–April 2012.
Jayne O'Donnell	"Hybrid Drivers May Save on Gas but New Tax Gotcha," *USA Today*, April 28, 2013.
Chris Paine	"5 Myths About Electric Cars," *Washington Post*, April 28, 2013.
Brian Palmer	"Even Hybrid and Plug-in Cars May Not Really Be Green," *Washington Post*, March 20, 2012.

Mark Phelan   "Are Drivers of Electric Cars Saints or Freeloaders?" *Detroit Free Press*, July 7, 2013.

Bruce Siceloff   "Hybrid, Electric Car Fees Could Help Make Up for Lost Taxes," *News Observer* (Raleigh, NC), May 27, 2013.

Margo Thorning   "Pull the Plug on Electric Car Subsidies," *Wall Street Journal*, March 24, 2011.

USA Today   "Uncle Sam Wants You—to Buy Electric Cars," August 3, 2010.

Daniel C. Vock   "State Gas Tax Could Be Replaced by Mileage," *USA Today*, August 1, 2013.

Joseph B. White   "Eyes on the Road: Electric Cars Struggle to Break Out of Niche," *Wall Street Journal*, September 26, 2012.

Brian Wynne   "Stop Bashing Electric Cars," *Politico*, April 18, 2012. www.politico.com.

Index

A

Advanced Technical Center, 52
Akerson, Dan, 78
Alternative fuel sources, 20–21
American Recovery and Reinvestment Act, 46
American Society of Civil Engineers, 87

B

Ballard, J.G., 88
Bastarache, Gerald, 80–83
Battery electric vehicles (BEVs)
  advantages and disadvantages, 59–60
  battery cost, 60–61
  displacing gasoline, 62–63
  economic advantages, 58–68
  overview, 7, 59
  policy impact, 64–66
  realistic assumptions, 63–64
  tax credit/subsidies for, 66–68
  See also Electric vehicles;
    Plug-in hybrid electric vehicles
Battery 2020 Project, 46
Battery technology, 12–13, 56
Bell, Perry, 11–14
Better Place, 17
Biodiesel, 21–22
Biomass to Liquid (BTL) diesel fuel, 21
Blumenauer, Earl, 85–88
Bomey, Nathan, 49–53

Brilliance Auto, 52
Buffett, Warren, 52

C

Carbon dioxide (CO_2) emissions
  capture and storage processes, 29
  combustion process, 28
  electric car comparisons, 26, 36
  electricity generation and, 38
  emissions-control devices, 27
  reduction of, 7
Carbon monoxide, 26
Carbon pricing, 67
Carnegie Mellon, 59
Chambers, Nick, 69–74
Charging infrastructure, 48
Chevy Cruze, 16, 55, 77
Chevy Volt
  battery packs for, 18, 19
  Chinese sales of, 52
  cleanliness of, 24
  gasoline use, 20
  leasing costs, 55
  tax credits for, 50
  US sales of, 16–17, 77
China, 43, 46
Chinese Association of Automobile Manufacturers, 50
Chinese not buying electric vehicles
  goals for, 51
  obstacles to, 49–50
  vehicle cost impact, 51–53
Chow, Namrita, 50

CleanTechnica, 7
Climate Central, 34
Climate change, 41–43
Coal consumption, 29, 39–40
Coburn, Tom, 87
CODA Automotive, 17
Congressional Budget Office, 65, 66
Congressional Research Service, 65
Culture Change (online magazine), 9

D

Defazio, Peter, 82
Denmark, 42, 82
Diesel fuel, 21–22, 71, 77

E

Edison2's Very Light Car, 57
Electric Drive Transportation Association, 8
Electricity, generation, 34–35
Electric vehicles (EVs)
    assault on, 70–71
    bright future of, 31–32
    Chinese not buying, 49–53
    circular reasoning, 72–73
    distorting demand for, 76–77
    electrons and, 28–31
    environmental benefits, 33–40
    global competitiveness of, 44–48
    government should not subsidize, 75–79
    government should subsidize, 69–74
    infrastructure for, 68
    market for, 78–79

mistakes/assumptions over, 71–72
    overview, 23–26, 69–70, 75–76
    sales of, 77–78
    service contract model for, 54–57
    vehicle emissions explained, 26–28
    See also Battery electric vehicles; Hybrid electric vehicles; Plug-in hybrid electric vehicles
Electrons, 28–31
Elon Musk, 17
Energy Policy (magazine), 67–68
Engelman, Robert, 41–43
Environmental benefits of electric cars
    changing landscape of, 34
    coal consumption and, 39–40
    comparison of, 35–36
    electricity generation, 38–39
    generation of electricity, 34–35
    MPG fuel economy, 36–37
    plug-in hybrids, 37–38
    state-to-state variations, 33–40
Epstein, Ethan, 84–88
Ethanol credit, 73
EV World (website), 25
E-ZPass (tracking system), 82

F

Federal Highway Trust Fund, 81–82
Fisker Automotive, 17, 24, 72
Ford Focus, 71
Ford Motor Co., 44–45
Fossil fuels, 35
Fuel efficiency standards, 9, 12

G

Gas tax, 85–86
General Motors Corp., 9, 44, 76
General Motors Corp., China, 50, 52
General Motors Spark EV, 19
Global competitiveness of electric cars
    emissions reductions, 47
    future of, 48
    manufacturing and, 45–47
    national security concerns, 47
    overview, 44–45
    reliance on oil, 45
    United States, 44–48
Global Positioning System (GPS), 81, 87
Green Car Journal (magazine), 24
Greenhouse gas emissions
    electric vehicles, 47
    Nissan Leaf, 34, 39
    overview, 25, 27
    significance of, 63

H

Harvard University, 8
High fructose corn syrup (HFCS), 21
High Voltage: The Fast Track to Plug In the Auto Industry (Motavalli), 10
Honda, 24
Honda Insight, 41–43
House Transportation & Infrastructure Committee, 82
HybridCars.com, 51
Hybrid electric vehicles (HEVs)
    battery technology, 12–13

climate change, 41–43
good sales of, 17–18
introduction, 7–10
overview, 11–12, 15–16
petroleum dependence, 11–14
poor sales of, 16–17
problem with, 18–20
reallocating resources for, 21–22
traditional cars vs., 15–22
See also Electric vehicles; Plug-in hybrid electric vehicles
Hydrocarbons, 26
Hydropower, 28

J

Jassim M. Jaidah Family Director of the Environment and Natural Resources Program, 8

K

Karma hybrid car, 17
Kenward, Alyson, 33–40
Kettering, Charles, 57
Kilowatt per hour (kWh) cost, 60–61
Kliesch, James, 23–32

L

LaHood, Ray, 86
Larson, Eric D., 33–40
LeBon, Bill, 9–10
Lee, Henry, 8–9
LoJack (tracking system), 82
Lundberg, Jan, 9, 10

M

Malone, Patrick, 86
McCain, John, 87
McManus, Walter, 9
Merkl, Steve, 52
Michalek, Jeremy, 58–68, 59
Mileage tax, for highway revenue
    environmental goals and,
        86–87
    is fair, 80–83
    is not fair, 84–88
    replacing gas tax, 85–86
Mitsubishi, 24
Moore, Bill, 25, 31
Motavalli, Jim, 10
Motor Trend (magazine), 24
MPG fuel economy, 36–37
Murphy, Debbie, 52

N

National security concerns, 47
National Surface Transportation
    Infrastructure Financing Com-
    mission, 81
Netherlands, 82
Nissan Leaf
    charging battery, 18, 19, 34,
        59–60
    cost of, 71–72
    efficiency of, 35
    future of, 31
    greenhouse gas emissions, 34,
        39
    MPG fuel economy, 36–37
    sales of, 16, 24, 76
    tax credits for, 50
Nissan North America, 31
Nitrogen oxides, 26
Nuclear power plants, 29

O

Oakland University, 9
Obama, Barack (administration)
    electric car goal, 8, 51
    electric car subsidies, 76
    fuel efficiency standards, 9
    mileage tax, 86
Oil imports, 76–77
On Star (GPS system), 82

P

Particulate matter (soot), 26, 28
Peny, Mark, 31
Perlow, Jason, 15–22
Perry, Mark J., 75–79
Petroleum dependence, 11–14
Pew Environment Group, 44–48
PluginCars.com, 70
Plug-in hybrid electric vehicles
    (PHEVs)
    cleanliness of, 25–26
    environmental benefits of,
        37–38
    introduction, 7
    recharging fuel, 12
    supply vs. demand, 13–14
Pollutants, 26–28
Pope, Carl, 54–57
Posawatz, Tony, 17

R

Rand Corp., 45
Reallocating resources for HEVs,
    21–22
*A Roadmap to Climate-Friendly
    Cars* report, 34, 39

S

Science Applications International
  Corporation (SAIC), 52
Service contract model for electric
  vehicles
    affordability of, 55–56
    appeal of, 54–57
    barriers to leasing, 56–57
    overview, 54–55
Shahan, Zachary, 7
Sierra Club, 9
Socia, Bob, 50
Solar energy, 13, 28
Sustainable Energy Institute, 9

T

Tax credit/subsidies, 50, 66–68, 70
TE Connectivity, 52
Tesla Model S, 18, 19
Tesla Motors
    Chinese dealerships, 52
    policy impact and, 65
    success of, 17, 24
TIME (magazine), 41
Toyota Prius, 18, 30, 35, 66
Toyota RAV4, 24
Traditional cars vs. hybrid electric
  vehicles, 15–22
Transit Connect van, 45

U

US Department of Energy, 30, 46
US Treasury Department, 85–86

V

Vehicle emissions explained, 26–28
Vehicle-miles traveled (VMT) tax.
  See Mileage tax, for highway rev-
  enue
Volkswagen Passat TDI, 21

W

Washington Post (newspaper),
  70–71
Wind energy, 28
Wynne, Brian, 8

X

XPRIZE winner, 57

Y

Yawitz, Daniel, 33–40

Z

Zero-emission vehicle, 66
Zhang, Yale, 51